S0-BBJ-330

OTHELLO
THE MOOR OF VENICE

OTHELLO
THE MOOR OF VENICE

William Shakespeare

Edited by Gerald Eades Bentley

BEDFORD / ST. MARTIN'S   Boston ◆ New York

For Bedford / St. Martin's

Developmental Editor: Emily Goodall
Marketing Manager: Richard Cadman
Text Design: Claire Seng-Niemoeller
Cover Design: Claire Jarvis
Composition: Stratford Publishing Services, Inc.
Printing and Binding: Malloy Lithographing, Inc.

President: Charles H. Christensen
Editorial Director: Joan E. Feinberg
Editor in Chief: Karen S. Henry
Director of Marketing: Karen Melton
Director of Editing, Design, and Production: Marcia Cohen
Managing Editor: Elizabeth M. Schaaf

Copyright © 2002 by Bedford /St. Martin's

All rights reserved. No part of this book may be reproduced, stored in a retrieval system, or transmitted in any form or by any means, electronic, mechanical, photocopying, recording, or otherwise, except as may be expressly permitted by the applicable copyright statutes or in writing by the Publisher.

Manufactured in the United States of America.

6 5 4 3 2 1

f e d c b a

For information, write: Bedford/St. Martin's, 75 Arlington Street, Boston, MA 02116 (617-399-4000)

ISBN: 0-312-40024-1

Acknowledgments

Text and notes from *Othello* by William Shakespeare, edited by Gerald Eades Bentley. Copyright © 1958, 1970 by Penguin Books; © 2000 by Penguin Putnam Inc. Used by permission of Penguin, a division of Penguin Putnam Inc.

OTHELLO THE MOOR OF VENICE

William Shakespeare

Edited by Gerald Eades Bentley

WILLIAM SHAKESPEARE (1564–1616)

Othello the Moor of Venice

1604

THE NAMES OF THE ACTORS

Othello, the Moor
Brabantio, [a Venetian senator,] father to Desdemona
Cassio, an honorable lieutenant [to Othello]
Iago, [Othello's ancient,] a villain
Roderigo, a gulled gentleman
Duke of Venice
Senators [of Venice]
Montano, governor of Cyprus
Lodovico and Gratiano, [kinsmen to Brabantio,] two noble Venetians
Sailors
Clowns
Desdemona, wife to Othello
Emilia, wife to Iago
Bianca, a courtesan
[Messenger, Herald, Officers, Venetian Gentlemen, Musicians, Attendants

SCENE: *Venice and Cyprus]*

ACT I

SCENE I: *A street in Venice.*

Enter Roderigo and Iago.

Roderigo: Tush, never tell me! I take it much unkindly
  That thou, Iago, who hast had my purse
  As if the strings were thine, shouldst know of this.°
Iago: 'Sblood,° but you'll not hear me!
  If ever I did dream of such a matter,   5
  Abhor me.
Roderigo: Thou told'st me thou didst hold him in thy hate.
Iago: Despise me if I do not. Three great ones of the city,
  In personal suit to make me his lieutenant,
  Off-capped to him;° and, by the faith of man,   10
  I know my price; I am worth no worse a place.
  But he, as loving his own pride and purposes,
  Evades them with a bombast circumstance.°
  Horribly stuffed with epithets of war;
  [And, in conclusion,]   15
  Nonsuits° my mediators; for, "Certes," says he,
  "I have already chose my officer."
  And what was he?
  Forsooth, a great arithmetician,°
  One Michael Cassio, a Florentine   20
  (A fellow almost damned in a fair wife°)
  That never set a squadron in the field,
  Nor the division of a battle knows
  More than a spinster; unless the bookish theoric,
  Wherein the togèd consuls can propose   25
  As masterly as he. Mere prattle without practice
  Is all his soldiership. But he, sir, had th' election;
  And I (of whom his eyes had seen the proof
  At Rhodes, at Cyprus, and on other grounds
  Christian and heathen) must be belee'd and calmed°   30
  By debitor and creditor; this counter-caster,°
  He, in good time, must his lieutenant be,
  And I — God bless the mark! — his Moorship's ancient.°
Roderigo: By heaven, I rather would have been his hangman.
Iago: Why, there's no remedy; 'tis the curse of service.   35
  Preferment goes by letter and affection,°
  And not by old gradation, where each second
  Stood heir to th' first. Now, sir, be judge yourself,
  Whether I in any just term am affined°

Act I, Scene I.   3 *this:* I.e., Desdemona's elopement.   4 *'Sblood:* By God's blood.
10 *him:* I.e., Othello.   13 *a bombast circumstance:* Pompous circumlocutions.   16 *Nonsuits:*
Rejects.   19 *arithmetician:* Theoretician.   21 *almost . . . wife:* (An obscure allusion; Cassio
is unmarried, but see IV.i.12).   30 *belee'd and calmed:* Left in the lurch.   31 *counter-caster:*
Bookkeeper.   33 *ancient:* Ensign.   36 *affection:* Favoritism.   39 *affined:* Obliged.

To love the Moor.
Roderigo: I would not follow him then.   40
Iago: O, sir, content you;
     I follow him to serve my turn upon him.
     We cannot all be masters, nor all masters
     Cannot be truly followed. You shall mark
     Many a duteous and knee-crooking knave   45
     That, doting on his own obsequious bondage,
     Wears out his time, much like his master's ass,
     For naught but provender; and when he's old, cashiered.°
     Whip me such honest knaves! Others there are
     Who, trimmed° in forms and visages of duty,   50
     Keep yet their hearts attending on themselves;
     And, throwing but shows of service on their lords,
     Do well thrive by them, and when they have lined their coats,
     Do themselves homage. These fellows have some soul;
     And such a one do I profess myself. For, sir,   55
     It is as sure as you are Roderigo,
     Were I the Moor, I would not be Iago.
     In following him, I follow but myself;
     Heaven is my judge, not I for love and duty,
     But seeming so, for my peculiar end;   60
     For when my outward action doth demonstrate
     The native act and figure of my heart°
     In compliment extern,° 'tis not long after
     But I will wear my heart upon my sleeve
     For daws to peck at; I am not what I am.   65
Roderigo: What a full fortune does the thick-lips° owe°
     If he can carry't thus!
Iago: Call up her father,
     Rouse him. Make after him, poison his delight,
     Proclaim him in the streets. Incense her kinsmen,
     And though he in a fertile climate dwell,   70
     Plague him with flies; though that his joy be joy,
     Yet throw such changes of vexation on't
     As it may lose some color.
Roderigo: Here is her father's house. I'll call aloud.
Iago: Do, with like timorous° accent and dire yell   75
     As when, by night and negligence, the fire
     Is spied in populous cities.
Roderigo: What, ho, Brabantio! Signior Brabantio, ho!
Iago: Awake! What, ho, Brabantio! Thieves! thieves! thieves!
     Look to your house, your daughter, and your bags!   80
     Thieves! thieves!

Brabantio at a window.°

48 *cashiered:* Turned off.   50 *trimmed:* Dressed up.   62 *The . . . heart:* What I really believe and intend.   63 *compliment extern:* Outward appearance.   66 *thick-lips:* An Elizabethan epithet for blacks, including Moors; *owe:* Own.   75 *timorous:* Terrifying.   *Brabantio at a window:* (added from quarto).

Brabantio (above): What is the reason of this terrible summons?
    What is the matter there?
Roderigo: Signior, is all your family within?
Iago: Are your doors locked?
Brabantio: Why, wherefore ask you this?   85
Iago: Zounds, sir, y' are robbed! For shame, put on your gown!
    Your heart is burst; you have lost half your soul.
    Even now, now, very now, an old black ram
    Is tupping your white ewe. Arise, arise!
    Awake the snorting° citizens with the bell.   90
    Or else the devil will make a grandsire of you.
    Arise, I say!
Brabantio: What, have you lost your wits?
Roderigo: Most reverend signior, do you know my voice?
Brabantio: Not I. What are you?   95
Roderigo: My name is Roderigo.
Brabantio: The worser welcome!
    I have charged thee not to haunt about my doors.
    In honest plainness thou hast heard me say
    My daughter is not for thee; and now, in madness,
    Being full of supper and distemp'ring draughts,   100
    Upon malicious knavery dost thou come
    To start my quiet.
Roderigo: Sir, sir, sir —
Brabantio: But thou must needs be sure
    My spirit and my place have in them power   105
    To make this bitter to thee.
Roderigo: Patience, good sir.
Brabantio: What tell'st thou me of robbing? This is Venice;
    My house is not a grange.°
Roderigo: Most grave Brabantio,
    In simple and pure soul I come to you.
Iago: Zounds, sir, you are one of those that will not serve God if the devil   110
    bid you. Because we come to do you service, and you think we are ruf-
    fians, you'll have your daughter covered with a Barbary horse; you'll
    have your nephews° neigh to you; you'll have coursers for cousins, and
    gennets for germans.°
Brabantio: What profane wretch art thou?   115
Iago: I am one, sir, that comes to tell you your daughter and the Moor are
    now making the beast with two backs.
Brabantio: Thou are a villain.
Iago: You are — a senator.
Brabantio: This thou shalt answer. I know thee, Roderigo.
Roderigo: Sir, I will answer anything. But I beseech you,   120
    If 't be your pleasure and most wise consent,
    As partly I find it is, that your fair daughter,

---

90 *snorting:* snoring.   108 *grange:* Isolated farmhouse.   113 *nephews:* I.e., grandsons.
114 *gennets for germans:* Spanish horses for near kinsmen.

At this odd-even° and dull watch o' th' night,
Transported, with no worse nor better guard
But with a knave of common hire, a gondolier,   125
To the gross clasps of a lascivious Moor —
If this be known to you, and your allowance,°
We then have done you bold and saucy wrongs;
But if you know not this, my manners tell me
We have your wrong rebuke. Do not believe   130
That, from the sense° of all civility,
I thus would play and trifle with your reverence.
Your daughter, if you have not given her leave,
I say again, hath made a gross revolt,
Tying her duty, beauty, wit, and fortunes   135
In an extravagant and wheeling° stranger
Of here and everywhere. Straight satisfy yourself.
If she be in her chamber, or your house,
Let loose on me the justice of the state
For thus deluding you.
Brabantio: Strike on the tinder, ho!   140
Give me a taper! Call up all my people!
This accident° is not unlike my dream.
Belief of it oppresses me already.
Light, I say! light!   *Exit [above].*
Iago: Farewell, for I must leave you.
It seems not meet, nor wholesome to my place,   145
To be produced — as, if I stay, I shall —
Against the Moor. For I do know the state,
However this may gall him with some check,°
Cannot with safety cast° him; for he's embarked
With such loud reason to the Cyprus wars,   150
Which even now stand in act,° that for their souls
Another of his fathom° they have none
To lead their business; in which regard,
Though I do hate him as I do hell-pains,
Yet, for necessity of present life,   155
I must show out a flag and sign of love,
Which is indeed but sign. That you shall surely find him,
Lead to the Sagittary° the raisèd search;
And there will I be with him. So farewell.   *Exit.*
Enter [below] Brabantio in his nightgown,° and Servants with torches.

Brabantio: It is too true an evil. Gone she is;   160
And what's to come of my despisèd time
Is naught but bitterness. Now, Roderigo,
Where didst thou see her? — O unhappy girl! —

---

123 *odd-even:* Between night and morning.   127 *allowance:* Approval.   131 *from the sense:*
In violation.   136 *extravagant and wheeling:* Expatriate and roving.   142 *accident:* Occur-
rence.   148 *check:* Reprimand.   149 *cast:* Discharge.   151 *stand in act:* Are going on.
152 *fathom:* Capacity.   158 *Sagittary:* An inn.   *nightgown:* Dressing gown.

With the Moor, say'st thou? — Who would be a father? —
How didst thou know 'twas she! — O, she deceives me   165
Past thought! — What said she to you? — Get moe° tapers!
Raise all my kindred! — Are they married, think you?
Roderigo: Truly I think they are.
Brabantio: O heaven! How got she out? O treason of the blood!
Fathers, from hence trust not your daughters' minds   170
By what you see them act. Is there not charms
By which the property° of youth and maidhood
May be abused? Have you not read, Roderigo,
Of some such thing?
Roderigo: Yes, sir, I have indeed.
Brabantio: Call up my brother. — O, would you had had her! —   175
Some one way, some another. — Do you know
Where we may apprehend her and the Moor?
Roderigo: I think I can discover him, if you please
To get good guard and go along with me.
Brabantio: I pray you lead on. At every house I'll call;   180
I may command at most. — Get weapons, ho!
And raise some special officers of night. —
On, good Roderigo; I'll deserve° your pains.   *Exeunt.*

SCENE II: *Before the lodgings of Othello.*

Enter Othello, Iago, and Attendants with torches.

Iago: Though in the trade of war I have slain men,
Yet do I hold it very stuff o' th' conscience
To do no contrived murther. I lack iniquity
Sometimes to do me service. Nine or ten times
I had thought t' have yerked° him here under the ribs.   5
Othello: 'Tis better as it is.
Iago: Nay, but he prated,
And spoke such scurvy and provoking terms
Against your honor
That with the little godliness I have
I did full hard forbear him. But I pray you, sir,   10
Are you fast° married? Be assured of this,
That the magnifico° is much beloved,
And hath in his effect a voice potential°
As double° as the Duke's. He will divorce you,
Or put upon you what restraint and grievance   15
The law, with all his might to enforce it on,
Will give him cable.
Othello: Let him do his spite.
My services which I have done the signiory°

---

166 *moe:* More.   172 *property:* Nature.   183 *deserve:* Show gratitude for.   **Scene II.**
5 *yerked:* Stabbed.   11 *fast:* Securely.   12 *magnifico:* Grandee (Brabantio).   13 *poten-*
tial: Powerful.   14 *double:* Doubly influential.   18 *signiory:* Venetian government.

Shall out-tongue his complaints. 'Tis yet to know°—
Which, when I know that boasting is an honor,   20
I shall promulgate—I fetch my life and being
From men of royal siege;° and my demerits°
May speak unbonneted to as proud a fortune
As this that I have reached.° For know, Iago,
But that I love the gentle Desdemona,   25
I would not my unhousèd° free condition
Put into circumscription and confine
For the sea's worth. But look what lights come yond?

Iago: Those are the raisèd father and his friends.
      You were best go in.

Othello: Not I; I must be found.   30
      My parts, my title, and my perfect soul°
      Shall manifest me rightly. Is it they?

Iago: By Janus, I think no.

      Enter Cassio, with torches, Officers.

Othello: The servants of the Duke, and my lieutenant.
      The goodness of the night upon you, friends!   35
      What is the news?

Cassio: The Duke does greet you, general;
      And he requires your haste-post-haste appearance
      Even on the instant.

Othello: What's the matter, think you?

Cassio: Something from Cyprus, as I may divine.
      It is a business of some heat. The galleys   40
      Have sent a dozen sequent° messengers
      This very night at one another's heels,
      And many of the consuls, raised and met,
      Are at the Duke's already. You have been hotly called for;
      When, being not at your lodging to be found,   45
      The Senate hath sent about three several quests
      To search you out.

Othello: 'Tis well I am found by you.
      I will but spend a word here in the house,
      And go with you.   [*Exit*]

Cassio: Ancient, what makes he here?

Iago: Faith, he to-night hath boarded a land carack.°   50
      If it prove lawful prize, he's made for ever.

Cassio: I do not understand.

Iago: He's married.

Cassio: To who?

      [*Enter Othello.*]

---

19 *yet to know:* Still not generally known.   22 *siege:* Rank; *demerits:* Deserts.   23–24 *May speak...reached:* Are equal, I modestly assert, to those of Desdemona's family.   26 *unhousèd:* Unrestrained.   31 *perfect soul:* Stainless conscience.   41 *sequent:* Consecutive.   50 *carack:* Treasure ship.

Iago: Marry, to — Come, captain, will you go?
Othello: Have with you.
Cassio: Here comes another troop to seek for you.

    Enter Brabantio, Roderigo, and others with lights and weapons.

Iago: It is Brabantio. General, be advised.   55
    He comes to bad intent.
Othello: Holla! stand there!
Roderigo: Signior, it is the Moor.
Brabantio: Down with him, thief!

    [They draw on both sides.]

Iago: You, Roderigo! Come, sir, I am for you.
Othello: Keep up° your bright swords, for the dew will rust them.
    Good signior, you shall more command with years   60
    Than with your weapons.
Brabantio: O thou foul thief, where hast thou stowed my daughter?
    Damned as thou art, thou hast enchanted her!
    For I'll refer me to all things of sense,
    If she in chains of magic were not bound,   65
    Whether a maid so tender, fair, and happy,
    So opposite to marriage that she shunned
    The wealthy curlèd darlings of our nation,
    Would ever have, t' incur a general mock,
    Run from her guardage to the sooty bosom   70
    Of such a thing as thou — to fear, not to delight.
    Judge me the world if 'tis not gross in sense°
    That thou hast practiced on her with foul charms,
    Abused her delicate youth with drugs or minerals
    That weaken motion.° I'll have't disputed on;   75
    'Tis probable, and palpable to thinking.
    I therefore apprehend and do attach° thee
    For an abuser of the world, a practicer
    Of arts inhibited and out of warrant.
    Lay hold upon him. If he do resist,   80
    Subdue him at his peril.
Othello: Hold your hands,
    Both you of my inclining and the rest.
    Were it my cue to fight, I should have known it
    Without a prompter. Where will you that I go
    To answer this your charge?
Brabantio: To prison, till fit time   85
    Of law and course of direct session°
    Call thee to answer.
Othello: What if I do obey?
    How may the Duke be therewith satisfied,
    Whose messengers are here about my side

---

59 *Keep up:* I.e., sheath.   72 *gross in sense:* Obvious.   75 *motion:* Perception.   77 *at-*
tach: Arrest.   86 *direct session:* Regular trial.

Upon some present business of the state   90
　　To bring me to him?
Officer:　　　　　　　'Tis true, most worthy signior.
　　The Duke's in council, and your noble self
　　I am sure is sent for.
Brabantio:　　　　　　　How? The Duke in council?
　　In this time of the night? Bring him away.
　　Mine's not an idle° cause. The Duke himself,   95
　　Or any of my brothers of the state,
　　Cannot but feel this wrong as 'twere their own;
　　For if such actions may have passage free,
　　Bondslaves and pagans shall our statesmen be.   *Exeunt.*

Scene III: *The Venetian Senate Chamber.*

　　Enter Duke and Senators, set at a table, with lights and Attendants.

Duke: There is no composition° in these news
　　That gives them credit.
1. Senator:　　　　　　　Indeed they are disproportioned.
　　My letters say a hundred and seven galleys.
Duke: And mine a hundred forty.
2. Senator:　　　　　　　And mine two hundred.
　　But though they jump° not on a just account—   5
　　As in these cases where the aim° reports
　　'Tis oft with difference—yet do they all confirm
　　A Turkish fleet, and bearing up to Cyprus.
Duke: Nay, it is possible enough to judgment.
　　I do not so secure me° in the error   10
　　But the main article° I do approve°
　　In fearful sense.
Sailor (within):　　　What, ho! what, ho! what, ho!
Officer: A messenger from the galleys.

　　Enter Sailor.

Duke:　　　　　　　　　Now, what's the business?
Sailor: The Turkish preparation makes for Rhodes.
　　So was I bid report here to the state   15
　　By Signior Angelo.
Duke: How say you by this change?
1. Senator:　　　　　　　This cannot be
　　By no assay° of reason. 'Tis a pageant
　　To keep us in false gaze.° When we consider
　　Th' importancy of Cyprus to the Turk,   20
　　And let ourselves again but understand
　　That, as it more concerns the Turk than Rhodes,

---

95 *idle:* Trifling.　　**Scene III.**　　1 *composition:* Consistency.　　5 *jump:* Agree.　　6 *aim:*
Conjecture.　　10 *so secure me:* Take such comfort.　　11 *article:* Substance; *approve:* Accept.
18 *assay:* Test.　　19 *in false gaze:* Looking the wrong way.

So may he with more facile question bear° it,
For that it stands not in such warlike brace,°
But altogether lacks th' abilities   25
That Rhodes is dressed in — if we make thought of this,
We must not think the Turk is so unskillful
To leave that latest which concerns him first,
Neglecting an attempt of ease and gain
To wake and wage° a danger profitless.   30

Duke: Nay, in all confidence, he's not for Rhodes.
Officer: Here is more news.

    Enter a Messenger.

Messenger: The Ottomites, reverend and gracious,
    Steering with due course toward the isle of Rhodes,
    Have there injointed them with an after fleet.   35
1. Senator: Ay, so I thought. How many, as you guess?
Messenger: Of thirty sail; and now they do restem°
    Their backward course, bearing with frank appearance
    Their purposes toward Cyprus, Signior Montano,
    Your trusty and most valiant servitor,   40
    With his free duty recommends you thus,
    And prays you to believe him.
Duke: 'Tis certain then for Cyprus.
    Marcus Luccicos,° is not he in town?
1. Senator: He's now in Florence.   45
Duke: Write from us to him; post, post-haste dispatch.
1. Senator: Here comes Brabantio and the valiant Moor.

    Enter Brabantio, Othello, Cassio, Iago, Roderigo, and Officers.

Duke: Valiant Othello, we must straight employ you
    Against the general enemy Ottoman.   *[To Brabantio.]*
    I did not see you. Welcome, gentle signior.   50
    We lacked your counsel and your help to-night.
Brabantio: So did I yours. Good your grace, pardon me.
    Neither my place, nor aught I heard of business,
    Hath raised me from my bed; nor doth the general care
    Take hold on me; for my particular grief   55
    Is of so floodgate° and o'erbearing nature
    That it engluts° and swallows other sorrows,
    And it is still itself.
Duke: Why, what's the matter?
Brabantio: My daughter! O, my daughter!
All: Dead?
Brabantio: Ay, to me.
    She is abused, stol'n from me, and corrupted   60
    By spells and medicines bought of mountebanks;

---

23 *with . . . bear:* More easily capture.   24 *brace:* Posture of defense.   30 *wake and wage:* Rouse and risk.   37 *restem:* Steer again.   44 *Marcus Luccicos:* (Presumably a Venetian envoy).   56 *floodgate:* Torrential.   57 *engluts:* Devours.

> For nature so prepost'rously to err,
> Being not deficient,° blind, or lame of sense,
> Sans witchcraft could not.

Duke: Whoe'er he be that in this foul proceeding   65
> Hath thus beguiled your daughter of herself,
> And you of her, the bloody book of law
> You shall yourself read in the bitter letter
> After your own sense; yea, though our proper° son
> Stood in your action.°

Brabantio: Humbly I thank your grace.   70
> Here is the man—this Moor, whom now, it seems,
> Your special mandate for the state affairs
> Hath hither brought.

All: We are very sorry for't.

Duke [to Othello]: What, in your own part, can you say to this?

Brabantio: Nothing, but this is so.   75

Othello: Most potent, grave, and reverend signiors,
> My very noble, and approved° good masters,
> That I have ta'en away this old man's daughter,
> It is most true; true I have married her.
> The very head and front of my offending   80
> Hath this extent, no more. Rude° am I in my speech,
> And little blessed with the soft phrase of peace;
> For since these arms of mine had seven years' pith°
> Till now some nine moons wasted, they have used
> Their dearest action in the tented field;   85
> And little of this great world can I speak
> More than pertains to feats of broil and battle;
> And therefore little shall I grace my cause
> In speaking for myself. Yet, by your gracious patience,
> I will a round° unvarnished tale deliver   90
> Of my whole course of love—what drugs, what charms,
> What conjuration, and what mighty magic
> (For such proceeding am I charged withal)
> I won his daughter.

Brabantio: A maiden never bold;
> Of spirit so still and quiet that her motion   95
> Blushed° at herself; and she—in spite of nature,
> Of years, of country, credit, everything—
> To fall in love with what she feared to look on!
> It is a judgment maimed and most imperfect
> That will confess perfection so could err   100
> Against all rules of nature, and must be driven
> To find out practices° of cunning hell
> Why this should be. I therefore vouch° again

---

63 *deficient:* Feeble-minded.   69 *our proper:* My own.   70 *Stood in your action:* Were ac-
cused by you.   77 *approved:* Tested by experience.   81 *Rude:* Unpolished.   83 *pith:*
Strength.   90 *round:* Plain.   95–96 *her motion Blushed:* Her own emotions caused her to
blush.   102 *practices:* Plots.   103 *vouch:* Assert.

That with some mixtures pow'rful o'er the blood,°
Or with some dram, conjured to this effect,   105
He wrought upon her.
Duke: To vouch this is no proof,
    Without more certain and more overt test
    Than these thin habits° and poor likelihoods
    Of modern seeming° do prefer against him.
1. Senator: But, Othello, speak.   110
    Did you by indirect and forcèd° courses
    Subdue and poison this young maid's affections?
    Or came it by request, and such fair question°
    As soul to soul affordeth?
Othello: I do beseech you,
    Send for the lady to the Sagittary   115
    And let her speak of me before her father.
    If you do find me foul in her report,
    The trust, the office, I do hold of you
    Not only take away, but let your sentence
    Even fall upon my life.
Duke: Fetch Desdemona hither.   120
Othello: Ancient, conduct them; you best know the place.
                          Exit [Iago, with] two or three [Attendants].
    And till she come, as truly as to heaven
    I do confess the vices of my blood,
    So justly to your grave ears I'll present
    How I did thrive in this fair lady's love,   125
    And she in mine.
Duke: Say it, Othello.
Othello: Her father loved me, oft invited me;
    Still° questioned me the story of my life
    From year to year — the battles, sieges, fortunes   130
    That I have passed.
    I ran it through, even from my boyish days
    To th' very moment that he bade me tell it.
    Wherein I spoke of most disastrous chances,
    Of moving accidents by flood and field;   135
    Of hairbreadth scapes i' th' imminent deadly breach;
    Of being taken by the insolent foe
    And sold to slavery; of my redemption thence
    And portance° in my travels' history;
    Wherein of anters° vast and deserts idle,   140
    Rough quarries, rocks, and hills whose heads touch heaven,
    It was my hint° to speak — such was the process;
    And of the Cannibals that each other eat,
    The Anthropophagi,° and men whose heads

---

104 *blood:* Passions.   108 *thin habits:* Slight appearances.   109 *modern seeming:* Every-
day supposition.   111 *forcèd:* Violent.   113 *question:* Conversation.   129 *Still:* Contin-
ually.   139 *portance:* Behavior.   140 *anters:* Caves.   142 *hint:* Occasion.   144 *An-
thropophagi:* Man-eaters.

Do grow beneath their shoulders. This to hear   145
Would Desdemona seriously incline;
But still the house affairs would draw her thence;
Which ever as she could with haste dispatch,
She'ld come again, and with a greedy ear
Devour up my discourse. Which I observing,   150
Took once a pliant° hour, and found good means
To draw from her a prayer of earnest heart
That I would all my pilgrimage dilate,°
Whereof by parcels° she had something heard,
But not intentively.° I did consent,   155
And often did beguile her of her tears
When I did speak of some distressful stroke
That my youth suffered. My story being done,
She gave me for my pains a world of sighs.
She swore, i' faith, 'twas strange, 'twas passing strange;   160
'Twas pitiful, 'twas wondrous pitiful.
She wished she had not heard it; yet she wished
That heaven had made her such a man. She thanked me;
And bade me, if I had a friend that loved her,
I should but teach him how to tell my story,   165
And that would woo her. Upon this hint° I spake.
She loved me for the dangers I had passed,
And I loved her that she did pity them.
This only is the witchcraft I have used.
Here comes the lady. Let her witness it.   170

Enter Desdemona, Iago, Attendants.

Duke: I think this tale would win my daughter too.
Good Brabantio,
Take up this mangled matter at the best.
Men do their broken weapons rather use
Than their bare hands.
Brabantio: I pray you hear her speak.   175
If she confess that she was half the wooer,
Destruction on my head if my bad blame
Light on the man! Come hither, gentle mistress.
Do you perceive in all this noble company
Where most you owe obedience?
Desdemona: My noble father,   180
I do perceive here a divided duty.
To you I am bound for life and education;°
My life and education both do learn me
How to respect you: you are the lord of duty;
I am hitherto your daughter. But here's my husband;   185
And so much duty as my mother showed
To you, preferring you before her father,

---

151 *pliant:* Propitious.   153 *dilate:* Recount in full.   154 *parcels:* Portions.   155 *intentively:* With full attention.   166 *hint:* Opportunity.   182 *education:* Upbringing.

So much I challenge° that I may profess
Due to the Moor my lord.

Brabantio: God be with you! I have done.
Please it your grace, on to the state affairs.   190
I had rather to adopt a child than get° it.
Come hither, Moor.
I here do give thee that with all my heart
Which, but thou hast already, with all my heart
I would keep from thee. For your sake,° jewel,   195
I am glad at soul I have no other child;
For thy escape° would teach me tyranny,
To hang clogs on them. I have done, my lord.

Duke: Let me speak like yourself° and lay a sentence°
Which, as a grise° or step, may help these lovers   200
[Into your favor.]
When remedies are past, the griefs are ended
By seeing the worst, which late on hopes depended.
To mourn a mischief that is past and gone
Is the next way to draw new mischief on.   205
What cannot be preserved when fortune takes,
Patience her injury a mock'ry makes.
The robbed that smiles steals something from the thief;
He robs himself that spends a bootless grief.

Brabantio: So let the Turk of Cyprus us beguile: 210
We lose it not so long as we can smile.
He bears the sentence well that nothing bears
But the free comfort which from thence he hears;
But he bears both the sentence and the sorrow
That to pay grief must of poor patience borrow.   215
These sentences, to sugar, or to gall,
Being strong on both sides, are equivocal.
But words are words. I never yet did hear
That the bruisèd heart was piercèd through the ear.
Beseech you, now to the affairs of state.   220

Duke: The Turk with a most mighty preparation makes for Cyprus.
Othello, the fortitude° of the place is best known to you; and though
we have there a substitute of most allowed° sufficiency, yet opinion,° a
more sovereign mistress of effects, throws a more safer voice on you.
You must therefore be content to slubber° the gloss of your new   225
fortunes with this more stubborn and boist'rous expedition.

Othello: The tyrant custom, most grave senators,
Hath made the flinty and steel couch of war
My thrice-driven bed of down. I do agnize
A natural and prompt alacrity   230
I find in hardness;° and do undertake

---

188 *challenge:* Claim the right.   191 *get:* Beget.   195 *For your sake:* Because of you.
197 *escape:* Escapade.   199 *like yourself:* As you should; *sentence:* Maxim.   200 *grise:*
Step.   222 *fortitude:* Fortification.   223 *allowed:* Acknowledged; *opinion:* Public opinion.
225 *slubber:* Sully.   229-31 *agnize . . . hardness:* Recognize in myself a natural and easy re-
sponse to hardship.

These present wars against the Ottomites.
Most humbly, therefore, bending to your state,
I crave fit disposition for my wife,
Due reference of place, and exhibition,°   235
With such accommodation and besort°
As levels° with her breeding.
Duke: If you please,
Be't at her father's.
Brabantio: I will not have it so.
Othello: Nor I.
Desdemona: Nor I. I would not there reside,   240
To put my father in impatient thoughts
By being in his eye. Most gracious Duke,
To my unfolding lend your prosperous° ear,
And let me find a charter in your voice,
T' assist my simpleness.°   245
Duke: What would you, Desdemona?
Desdemona: That I did love the Moor to live with him,
My downright violence, and storm of fortunes,
May trumpet to the world. My heart's subdued
Even to the very quality of my lord.   250
I saw Othello's visage in his mind,
And to his honors and his valiant parts
Did I my soul and fortunes consecrate.
So that, dear lords, if I be left behind,
A moth of peace, and he go to the war,   255
The rites for which I love him are bereft me,
And I a heavy interim shall support
By his dear absence. Let me go with him.
Othello: Let her have your voice.
Vouch with me, heaven, I therefore beg it not   260
To please the palate of my appetite,
Not to comply with heat° — the young affects°
In me defunct — and proper satisfaction;
But to be free and bounteous to her mind;
And heaven defend your good souls that you think   265
I will your serious and great business scant
When she is with me. No, when light-winged toys
Of feathered Cupid seel° with wanton dullness
My speculative and officed instruments,°
That° my disports corrupt and taint my business,   270
Let housewives make a skillet of my helm,
And all indign° and base adversities
Make head against my estimation!°

---

235 *exhibition:* Allowance of money.   236 *besort:* Suitable company.   237 *levels:* Corre-
sponds.   243 *prosperous:* Favorable.   245 *simpleness:* Lack of skill.   262 *heat:* Passions;
young affects: Tendencies of youth.   268 *seel:* Blind.   269 *My . . . instruments:* My percep-
tive and responsible faculties.   270 *That:* So that.   272 *indign:* Unworthy.   273 *estimation:* Reputation.

Duke: Be it as you shall privately determine,
  Either for her stay or going. Th' affair cries haste,   275
  And speed must answer it.
I. Senator: You must away to-night.
Othello: With all my heart.
Duke: At nine i' th' morning here we'll meet again.
  Othello, leave some officer behind,
  And he shall our commission bring to you,   280
  With such things else of quality and respect
  As doth import° you.
Othello: So please your grace, my ancient;
  A man he is of honesty and trust
  To his conveyance I assign my wife,
  With what else needful your good grace shall think   285
  To be sent after me.
Duke: Let it be so.
  Good night to every one.
        [To Brabantio.]   And, noble signior,
  If virtue no delighted° beauty lack,
  Your son-in-law is far more fair than black.
I. Senator: Adieu, brave Moor. Use Desdemona well.   290
Brabantio: Look to her, Moor, if thou hast eyes to see:
  She has deceived her father, and may thee.
                    Exeunt [Duke, Senators, Officers, &c.].
Othello: My life upon her faith! — Honest Iago,
  My Desdemona must I leave to thee.
  I prithee let thy wife attend on her,   295
  And bring them after in the best advantage.°
  Come, Desdemona. I have but an hour
  Of love, of worldly matters and direction,
  To spend with thee. We must obey the time.
                    Exit Moor and Desdemona.
Roderigo: Iago, —   300
Iago: What say'st thou, noble heart?
Roderigo: What will I do, think'st thou?
Iago: Why, go to bed and sleep.
Roderigo: I will incontinently° drown myself.
Iago: If thou dost, I shall never love thee after. Why, thou silly gentleman!   305
Roderigo: It is silliness to live when to live is torment; and then have we a
  prescription to die when death is our physician.
Iago: O villainous! I have looked upon the world for four times seven
  years; and since I could distinguish betwixt a benefit and an injury, I
  never found man that knew how to love himself. Ere I would say I   310
  would drown myself for the love of a guinea hen, I would change my
  humanity with a baboon.
Roderigo: What should I do? I confess it is my shame to be so fond, but it is
  not in my virtue to amend it.

---

282 *import:* Concern.   288 *delighted:* Delightful.   296 *in the best advantage:* At the best
opportunity.   304 *incontinently:* Forthwith.

Iago: Virtue? a fig! 'Tis in ourselves that we are thus or thus. Our bodies 315
are our gardens, to which our wills are gardeners; so that if we will
plant nettles or sow lettuce, set hyssop and weed up thyme, supply it
with one gender° of herbs or distract it with many—either to have it
sterile with idleness or manured with industry—why, the power and
corrigible authority° of this lies in our wills. If the balance of our lives 320
had not one scale of reason to poise° another of sensuality, the blood
and baseness° of our natures would conduct us to most preposterous
conclusions. But we have reason to cool our raging motions,° our carnal strings, our unbitted° lusts; whereof I take this that you call love
to be a sect or scion.°   325

Roderigo: It cannot be.

Iago: It is merely a lust of the blood and a permission of the will. Come, be a
man! Drown thyself? Drown cats and blind puppies! I have professed
me thy friend, and I confess me knit to thy deserving with cables of per-
durable toughness. I could never better stead thee than now. Put money 330
in thy purse. Follow thou the wars; defeat thy favor° with an usurped
beard. I say, put money in thy purse. It cannot be that Desdemona
should long continue her love to the Moor—put money in thy purse—
nor he his to her. It was a violent commencement in her, and thou shalt
see an answerable sequestration°—put but money in thy purse. These 335
Moors are changeable in their wills—fill thy purse with money. The
food that to him now is as luscious as locusts shall be to him shortly as
bitter as coloquintida.° She must change for youth: when she is sated
with his body, she will find the error of her choice. [She must have
change, she must.] Therefore put money in thy purse. If thou wilt needs 340
damn thyself, do it a more delicate way than drowning. Make° all the
money thou canst. If sanctimony and a frail vow betwixt an erring° bar-
barian and a supersubtle Venetian be not too hard for my wits and all
the tribe of hell, thou shalt enjoy her. Therefore make money. A pox of
drowning thyself! 'Tis clean out of the way. Seek thou rather to be 345
hanged in compassing thy joy than to be drowned and go without her.

Roderigo: Wilt thou be fast to my hopes, if I depend on the issue?

Iago: Thou art sure of me. Go, make money. I have told thee often, and I
retell thee again and again, I hate the Moor. My cause is hearted;°
thine hath no less reason. Let us be conjunctive in our revenge against 350
him. If thou canst cuckold him, thou dost thyself a pleasure, me a
sport. There are many events in the womb of time, which will be deliv-
ered. Traverse,° go, provide thy money! We will have more of this to-
morrow. Adieu.

Roderigo: Where shall we meet i' th' morning?   355

Iago: At my lodging.

Roderigo: I'll be with thee betimes.

Iago: Go to, farewell—Do you hear, Roderigo?

---

318 *gender:* Species.   320 *corrigible authority:* Corrective power.   321 *poise:* Counterbal-
ance.   321–22 *blood and baseness:* Animal instincts.   323 *motions:* Appetites.   324 *un-
bitted:* Uncontrolled.   325 *sect or scion:* Offshoot, cutting.   331 *defeat thy favor:* Spoil thy
appearance.   335 *sequestration:* Estrangement.   338 *coloquintida:* A medicine.   341 *Make:*
Raise.   342 *erring:* Wandering.   349 *My cause is hearted:* My heart is in it.   353 *Traverse:* Forward march.

[*Roderigo:* What say you?
Iago: No more of drowning, do you hear?   360
Roderigo: I am changed.
Iago: Go to, farewell. Put money enough in your purse.]
Roderigo: I'll sell all my land.   *Exit.*
Iago: Thus do I ever make my fool my purse;
    For I mine own gained knowledge should profane   365
    If I would time expend with such a snipe°
    But for my sport and profit. I hate the Moor;
    And it is thought abroad that 'twixt my sheets
    H'as done my office. I know not if't be true;
    But I, for mere suspicion in that kind,   370
    Will do as if for surety. He holds me well;°
    The better shall my purpose work on him.
    Cassio's a proper man. Let me see now:
    To get his place, and to plume up° my will
    In double knavery—How, how?—Let's see:—   375
    After some time, to abuse Othello's ears
    That he is too familiar with his wife.
    He hath a person and a smooth dispose°
    To be suspected—framed to make women false.
    The Moor is of a free° and open nature   380
    That thinks men honest that but seem to be so;
    And will as tenderly be led by th' nose
    As asses are.
    I have't! It is engend'red! Hell and night
    Must bring this monstrous birth to the world's light.   *Exit.* 385

ACT II

Scene I: *An open place in Cyprus, near the harbor.*

   Enter Montano and two Gentlemen.

Montano: What from the cape can you discern at sea?
1. Gentleman: Nothing at all: it is a high-wrought flood.
    I cannot 'twixt the heaven and the main
    Descry a sail.
Montano: Methinks the wind hath spoke aloud at land;   5
    A fuller blast ne'er shook our battlements.
    If it hath ruffianed so upon the sea,
    What ribs of oak, when mountains melt on them,
    Can hold the mortise?° What shall we hear of this?
2. Gentleman: A segregation° of the Turkish fleet.   10
    For do but stand upon the foaming shore,

---

366 *snipe:* Fool.   371 *well:* In high regard.   374 *plume up:* Gratify.   378 *dispose:* Manner.   380 *free:* Frank.   **Act II, Scene I.**   9 *hold the mortise:* Hold their joints together.
10 *segregation:* Scattering.

The chidden billow seems to pelt the clouds;
The wind-shaked surge, with high and monstrous mane,
Seems to cast water on the burning Bear
And quench the Guards° of th' ever-fixèd pole.°   15
I never did like molestation° view
On the enchafèd flood.

Montano: If that the Turkish fleet
Be not ensheltered and embayed, they are drowned;
It is impossible to bear it out.

     Enter a third Gentleman.

3. Gentleman: News, lads! Our wars are done.   20
The desperate tempest hath so banged the Turks
That their designment halts.° A noble ship of Venice
Hath seen a grievous wrack and sufferance°
On most part of their fleet.

Montano: How? Is this true?

3. Gentleman: The ship is here put in,   25
A Veronesa;° Michael Cassio,
Lieutenant to the warlike Moor Othello,
Is come on shore; the Moor himself at sea,
And is in full commission here for Cyprus.

Montano: I am glad on't. 'Tis a worthy governor.   30

3. Gentleman: But his same Cassio, though he speak of comfort
Touching the Turkish loss, yet he looks sadly
And prays the Moor be safe, for they were parted
With foul and violent tempest.

Montano: Pray heaven he be;
For I have served him, and the man commands   35
Like a full soldier. Let's to the seaside, ho!
As well to see the vessel that's come in
As to throw out our eyes for brave Othello,
Even till we make the main and th' aerial blue
An indistinct regard.°

3. Gentleman: Come, let's do so;   40
For every minute is expectancy
Of more arrivance.

     Enter Cassio.

Cassio: Thanks, you the valiant of this warlike isle,
That so approve the Moor! O, let the heavens
Give him defense against the elements,
For I have lost him on a dangerous sea!   45

Montano: Is he well shipped?

Cassio: His bark is stoutly timbered, and his pilot
Of very expert and approved allowance;

---

15 *Guards:* Stars near the North Star; *pole:* Polestar.   16 *molestation:* Tumult.   22 *de-signment halts:* Plan is crippled.   23 *sufferance:* Disaster.   26 *Veronesa:* Ship furnished by Verona.   40 *An indistinct regard:* Indistinguishable.

Therefore my hopes, not surfeited to death,°   50
Stand in bold cure.°
     (Within.)   A sail, a sail, a sail!   *Enter a messenger.*
Cassio: What noise?
Messenger: The town is empty; on the brow o' th' sea
    Stand ranks of people, and they cry "A sail!"
Cassio: My hopes do shape him for the governor.   55

    A shot.

2. Gentleman: They do discharge their shot of courtesy:
    Our friends at least.
Cassio: I pray you, sir, go forth
    And give us truth who 'tis that is arrived.
2. Gentleman: I shall.   *Exit.*
Montano: But, good lieutenant, is your general wived?   60
Cassio: Most fortunately. He hath achieved a maid
    That paragons° description and wild fame;
    One that excels the quirks° of blazoning° pens,
    And in th' essential vesture of creation
    Does tire the ingener.°

    Enter Second Gentleman.

                How now? Who has put in?   65
2. Gentleman: 'Tis one Iago, ancient to the general.
Cassio: H'as had most favorable and happy speed:
    Tempests themselves, high seas, and howling winds,
    The guttered° rocks and congregated sands,
    Traitors ensteeped° to clog the guiltless keel,   70
    As having sense of beauty, do omit
    Their mortal° natures, letting go safely by
    The divine Desdemona.
Montano: What is she?
Cassio: She that I spake of, our great captain's captain,
    Left in the conduct of the bold Iago,   75
    Whose footing° here anticipates our thoughts
    A se'nnight's° speed. Great Jove, Othello guard,
    And swell his sail with thine own pow'rful breath,
    That he may bless this bay with his tall ship,
    Make love's quick pants in Desdemona's arms,   80
    Give renewed fire to our extincted spirits,
    [And bring all Cyprus comfort!]

    Enter Desdemona, Iago, Roderigo, and Emilia [with Attendants].

                  O, behold!
The riches of the ship is come on shore!

---

50 *surfeited to death:* Overindulged.   51 *in bold cure:* A good chance of fulfillment.   62 *paragons:* Surpasses.   63 *quirks:* Ingenuities; *blazoning:* Describing.   64–65 *And . . . ingener:* Merely to describe her as God made her exhausts her praiser.   69 *guttered:* Jagged.
70 *ensteeped:* Submerged.   72 *mortal:* Deadly.   76 *footing:* Landing.   77 *se'nnight's:* Week's.

    You men of Cyprus, let her have your knees.°
    Hail to thee, lady! and the grace of heaven,   85
    Before, behind thee, and on every hand,
    Enwheel thee round!
Desdemona: I thank you, valiant Cassio.
    What tidings can you tell me of my lord?
Cassio: He is not yet arrived; nor know I aught
    But that he's well and will be shortly here.   90
Desdemona: O but I fear! How lost you company?
Cassio: The great contention of the sea and skies
    Parted our fellowship.
      (Within.)   A sail, a sail! *[A shot.]*
                                     But hark. A sail!
2. Gentleman: They give their greeting to the citadel;
    This likewise is a friend.
Cassio: See for the news.   95
                                 [Exit Gentleman.]
    Good ancient, you are welcome.
      [To Emilia.]   Welcome, mistress. —
    Let it not gall your patience, good Iago,
    That I extend my manners. 'Tis my breeding
    That gives me this bold show of courtesy.
      [Kisses Emilia.°]

Iago: Sir, would she give you so much of her lips
    As of her tongue she oft bestows on me,   100
    You would have enough.
Desdemona: Alas, she has no speech!
Iago: In faith, too much.
    I find it still when I have list to sleep.
    Marry, before your ladyship, I grant,   105
    She puts her tongue a little in her heart
    And chides with thinking.
Emilia: You have little cause to say so.
Iago: Come on, come on! You are pictures out of doors,
    Bells in your parlors, wildcats in your kitchens,   110
    Saints in your injuries, devils being offended,
    Players in your housewifery,° and housewives° in your beds.
Desdemona: O, fie upon thee, slanderer!
Iago: Nay, it is true, or else I am a Turk:
    You rise to play, and go to bed to work.   115
Emilia: You shall not write my praise.
Iago: No, let me not.
Desdemona: What wouldst thou write of me, if thou shouldst praise me?
Iago: O gentle lady, do not put me to't,
    For I am nothing if not critical.
Desdemona: Come on, assay.° — There's one gone to the harbor?   120

---

84 *knees:* I.e., kneeling.   *Kisses Emilia:* (Kissing was a common Elizabethan form of social courtesy).   112 *housewifery:* Housekeeping; *housewives:* Hussies.   120 *assay:* Try.

Iago: Ay, madam.

Desdemona: I am not merry; but I do beguile
    The thing I am by seeming otherwise. —
    Come, how wouldst thou praise me?

Iago: I am about it; but indeed my invention   125
    Comes from my pate as birdlime° does from frieze°—
    It plucks out brains and all. But my Muse labors,
    And thus she is delivered:
    If she be fair and wise, fairness and wit—
    The one's for use, the other useth it.   130

Desdemona: Well praised! How if she be black° and witty?

Iago: If she be black, and thereto have a wit,
    She'll find a white that shall her blackness fit.

Desdemona: Worse and worse!

Emilia: How if fair and foolish?   135

Iago: She never yet was foolish that was fair,
    For even her folly° helped her to an heir.

Desdemona: These are old fond° paradoxes to make fools laugh i' th' ale-
    house. What miserable praise hast thou for her that's foul° and foolish?

Iago: There's none so foul, and foolish thereunto,   140
    But does foul pranks which fair and wise ones do.

Desdemona: O heavy ignorance! Thou praisest the worst best. But what
    praise couldst thou bestow on a deserving woman indeed—one that
    in the authority of her merit did justly put on the vouch° of very
    malice itself?   145

Iago: She that was ever fair, and never proud;
    Had tongue at will, and yet was never loud;
    Never lacked gold, and yet went never gay;
    Fled from her wish, and yet said "Now I may";
    She that, being ang'red, her revenge being nigh,   150
    Bade her wrong stay, and her displeasure fly;
    She that in wisdom never was so frail
    To change the cod's head for the salmon's tail;°
    She that could think, and ne'er disclose her mind;
    See suitors following, and not look behind: 155
    She was a wight (if ever such wight were)—

Desdemona: To do what?

Iago: To suckle fools and chronicle small beer.°

Desdemona: O most lame and impotent conclusion! Do not learn of him,
    Emilia, though he be thy husband. How say you, Cassio? Is he not a 160
    most profane and liberal° counsellor?

Cassio: He speaks home,° madam. You may relish him more in the soldier
    than in the scholar.

Iago [aside]: He takes her by the palm. Ay, well said, whisper! With as little
    a web as this will I ensnare as great a fly as Cassio. Ay, smile upon her, 165

---

126 *birdlime:* A sticky paste; *frieze:* Rough cloth.   131 *black:* Brunette.   137 *folly:* Wan-
tonness.   138 *fond:* Foolish.   139 *foul:* Ugly.   144 *put on the vouch:* Compel the approval.   153 *To . . . tail:* I.e., to exchange the good for the poor but expensive.   158 *chronicle small beer:* Keep petty household accounts.   161 *profane and liberal:* Worldly and
licentious.   162 *home:* Bluntly.

do! I will gyve thee in thine own courtship.° — You say true; 'tis so, indeed! — If such tricks as these strip you out of your lieutenantry, it
had been better you had not kissed your three fingers so oft — which
now again you are most apt to play the sir° in. Very good! well kissed!
an excellent courtesy! 'Tis so, indeed. Yet again your fingers to your   170
lips? Would they were clyster pipes° for your sake! *(Trumpet within.)*
The Moor! I know his trumpet.
Cassio: 'Tis truly so.
Desdemona: Let's meet him and receive him.
Cassio: Lo, where he comes.   175

    Enter Othello and Attendants.

Othello: O my fair warrior!
Desdemona: My dear Othello!
Othello: It gives me wonder great as my content
  To see you here before me. O my soul's joy!
  If after every tempest come such calms,
  May the winds blow till they have wakened death!   180
  And let the laboring bark climb hills of seas
  Olympus-high, and duck again as low
  As hell's from heaven! If it were now to die,
  'Twere now to be most happy;° for I fear
  My soul hath her content so absolute   185
  That not another comfort like to this
  Succeeds in unknown fate.
Desdemona: The heavens forbid
  But that our loves and comforts should increase
  Even as our days do grow.
Othello: Amen to that, sweet powers!
  I cannot speak enough of this content;   190
  It stops me here; it is too much of joy.
  And this, and this, the greatest discords be

    They kiss.

  That e'er our hearts shall make!
Iago [aside]:   O, you are well tuned now!
  But I'll set down° the pegs that make this music,
  As honest as I am.
Othello: Come, let us to the castle.   195
  News, friends! Our wars are done; the Turks are drowned.
  How does my old acquaintance of this isle? —
  Honey, you shall be well desired° in Cyprus;
  I have found great love amongst them. O my sweet,
  I prattle out of fashion, and I dote   200
  In mine own comforts. I prithee, good Iago,
  Go to the bay and disembark my coffers.

---

166 *gyve . . . courtship:* Manacle you by means of your courtly manners.   169 *sir:* Courtly
gentleman.   171 *clyster pipes:* Syringes.   184 *happy:* Fortunate.   194 *set down:* Loosen.
198 *well desired:* Warmly welcomed.

Bring thou the master° to the citadel;
He is a good one, and his worthiness
Does challenge° much respect. — Come, Desdemona,   205
Once more well met at Cyprus.

> *Exit Othello [with all but Iago and Roderigo].*

Iago [to an Attendant, who goes out]: Do thou meet me presently at the harbor. *[To Roderigo.]* Come hither. If thou be'st valiant (as they say base
men being in love have then a nobility in their natures more than is
native to them), list me. The lieutenant to-night watches on the court   210
of guard.° First, I must tell thee this: Desdemona is directly in love
with him.

Roderigo: With him? Why, 'tis not possible.

Iago: Lay thy finger thus,° and let thy soul be instructed. Mark me with what
violence she first loved the Moor, but for bragging and telling her fan-   215
tastical lies; and will she love him still for prating? Let not thy discreet
heart think it. Her eye must be fed; and what delight shall she have to
look on the devil? When the blood is made dull with the act of sport,
there should be, again to inflame it and to give satiety a fresh appetite,
loveliness in favor, sympathy in years, manners, and beauties; all which   220
the Moor is defective in. Now for want of these required conveniences,° her delicate tenderness will find itself abused, begin to heave
the gorge,° disrelish and abhor the Moor. Very nature will instruct her
in it and compel her to some second choice. Now, sir, this granted — as
it is a most pregnant° and unforced position — who stands so eminent   225
in the degree of this fortune as Cassio does? A knave very voluble; no
further conscionable° than in putting on the mere form of civil and
humane° seeming for the better compassing of his salt° and most hid-
den loose affection? Why, none! why, none! A slipper° and subtle knave;
a finder-out of occasions; that has an eye can stamp and counterfeit   230
advantages, though true advantage never present itself; a devilish
knave! Besides, the knave is handsome, young, and hath all those req-
uisites in him that folly and green minds look after. A pestilent complete knave! and the woman hath found him already.

Roderigo: I cannot believe that in her; she's full of most blessed condition.°   235

Iago: Blessed fig's-end! The wine she drinks is made of grapes. If she had
been blessed, she would never have loved the Moor. Blessed pudding!
Didst thou not see her paddle with the palm of his hand? Didst not
mark that?

Roderigo: Yes, that I did; but that was but courtesy.   240

Iago: Lechery, by this hand! an index and obscure prologue to the history
of lust and foul thoughts. They met so near with their lips that their
breaths embraced together. Villainous thoughts, Roderigo! When
these mutualities° so marshal the way, hard at hand comes the master
and main exercise, th' incorporate° conclusion. Pish! But, sir, be you   245

---

203 *master:* Ship captain.   205 *challenge:* Deserve.   210–11 *court of guard:* Headquarters.
214 *thus:* I.e., on your lips.   221–22 *conveniences:* Compatibilities.   222–23 *heave the gorge:*
Be nauseated.   225 *pregnant:* Evident.   227 *conscionable:* Conscientious   228 *humane:*
Polite;   *salt:* Lecherous.   229 *slipper:* Slippery.   235 *condition:* Character.   244 *mutu-
alities:* Exchanges.   245 *incorporate:* Carnal.

ruled by me: I have brought you from Venice. Watch you to-night; for the command, I'll lay't upon you. Cassio knows you not. I'll not be far from you: do you find some occasion to anger Cassio, either by speaking too loud, or tainting° his discipline, or from what other course you please which the time shall more favorably minister.　　　250

Roderigo: Well.

Iago: Sir, he's rash and very sudden in choler,° and haply with his truncheon may strike at you. Provoke him that he may; for even out of that will I cause these of Cyprus to mutiny; whose qualification° shall come into no true taste° again but by the displanting of Cassio. So shall you　255 have a shorter journey to your desires by the means I shall then have to prefer° them; and the impediment most profitably removed without the which there were no expectation of our prosperity.

Roderigo: I will do this if you can bring it to any opportunity.

Iago: I warrant thee. Meet me by and by at the citadel; I must fetch his　260 necessaries ashore. Farewell.

Roderigo: Adieu.　　　　　　　　　　　　　　　　　　　　　*Exit.*

Iago: That Cassio loves her, I do well believe't;
　That she loves him, 'tis apt° and of great credit.
　The Moor, howbeit that I endure him not,　　　　　　　　265
　Is of a constant, loving, noble nature,
　And I dare think he'll prove to Desdemona
　A most dear husband. Now I do love her too;
　Not out of absolute lust, though peradventure
　I stand accountant° for as great a sin,　　　　　　　　　270
　But partly led to diet° my revenge,
　For that I do suspect the lusty Moor
　Hath leaped into my seat; the thought whereof
　Doth, like a poisonous mineral, gnaw my inwards;
　And nothing can or shall content my soul　　　　　　　275
　Till I am evened with him, wife for wife;
　Or failing so, yet that I put the Moor
　At least into a jealousy so strong
　That judgment cannot cure. Which thing to do,
　If this poor trash of Venice, whom I trash°　　　　　　280
　For° his quick hunting, stand the putting on,°
　I'll have our Michael Cassio on the hip,°
　Abuse him to the Moor in the rank garb°
　(For I fear Cassio with my nightcap too),
　Make the Moor thank me, love me, and reward me　　285
　For making him egregiously an ass
　And practicing upon° his peace and quiet
　Even to madness. 'Tis here, but yet confused:
　Knavery's plain face is never seen till used.　　　　　*Exit.*

---

249 *tainting:* Discrediting.　252 *sudden in choler:* Violent in anger.　254 *qualification:* Appeasement.　255 *true taste:* Satisfactory state.　257 *prefer:* Advance.　264 *apt:* Probable.　270 *accountant:* Accountable.　271 *diet:* Feed.　280 *I trash:* I weight down (in order to keep under control).　281 *For:* In order to develop; *stand the putting on:* Responds to my inciting.　282 *on the hip:* At my mercy.　283 *rank garb:* Gross manner.　287 *practicing upon:* Plotting against.

SCENE II: *A street in Cyprus.*

Enter Othello's Herald, with a proclamation.

Herald: It is Othello's pleasure, our noble and valiant general, that, upon
certain tidings now arrived, importing the mere perdition° of the
Turkish fleet, every man put himself into triumph; some to dance,
some to make bonfires, each man to what sport and revels his addic-
tion leads him. For, besides these beneficial news, it is the celebration   5
of his nuptial. So much was his pleasure should be proclaimed. All of-
fices° are open, and there is full liberty of feasting from the present
hour of five till the bell have told eleven. Heaven bless the isle of
Cyprus and our noble general Othello!   *Exit.*

SCENE III: *The Cyprian Castle.*

Enter Othello, Desdemona, Cassio, and Attendants.

Othello: Good Michael, look you to the guard to-night.
Let's teach ourselves that honorable stop,
Not to outsport discretion.
Cassio: Iago hath direction what to do;
But not withstanding, with my personal eye   5
Will I look to't.
Othello: Iago is most honest.
Michael, good night. To-morrow with your earliest
Let me have speech with you.
    [To Desdemona.]   Come, my dear love.
The purchase made, the fruits are to ensue;
That profit's yet to come 'tween me and you. —   10
Good night.
                    Exit [Othello with Desdemona and Attendants].

Enter Iago.

Cassio: Welcome, Iago. We must to the watch.
Iago: Not this hour, lieutenant; 'tis not yet ten o' th' clock. Our general
cast° us thus early for the love of his Desdemona; who let us not
therefore blame. He hath not yet made wanton the night with her,   15
and she is sport for Jove.
Cassio: She's a most exquisite lady.
Iago: And, I'll warrant her, full of game.
Cassio: Indeed, she's a most fresh and delicate creature.
Iago: What an eye she has! Methinks it sounds a parley to provocation.   20
Cassio: An inviting eye; and yet methinks right modest.
Iago: And when she speaks, is it not an alarum to love?
Cassio: She is indeed perfection.
Iago: Well, happiness to their sheets! Come, lieutenant, I have a stoup° of
wine, and here without are a brace of Cyprus gallants that would fain   25
have a measure to the health of black Othello.

***

Scene II.   2 *mere perdition:* Complete destruction.   6–7 *offices:* Kitchens and store-
rooms.   **Scene III.**   14 *cast:* Dismissed.   24 *stoup:* Two-quart tankard.

Cassio: Not to-night, good Iago. I have very poor and unhappy brains for
 drinking; I could well wish courtesy would invent some other custom
 of entertainment.

Iago: O, they are our friends. But one cup! I'll drink for you.   30

Cassio: I have drunk but one cup to-night, and that was craftily qualified°
 too; and behold what innovation° it makes here. I am unfortunate in
 the infirmity and dare not task my weakness with any more.

Iago: What, man! 'Tis a night of revels: the gallants desire it.

Cassio: Where are they?   35

Iago: Here at the door; I pray you call them in.

Cassio: I'll do't, but it dislikes me.   *Exit.*

Iago: If I can fasten but one cup upon him
 With that which he hath drunk to-night already,
 He'll be as full of quarrel and offense   40
 As my young mistress' dog. Now my sick fool Roderigo,
 Whom love hath turned almost the wrong side out,
 To Desdemona hath to-night caroused
 Potations pottle-deep;° and he's to watch.
 Three lads of Cyprus—noble swelling spirits,   45
 That hold their honors in a wary distance,°
 The very elements° of this warlike isle—
 Have I to-night flustered with flowing cups,
 And they watch too. Now, 'mongst this flock of drunkards
 Am I to put our Cassio in some action   50
 That may offend the isle.

Enter Cassio, Montano, and Gentlemen [; Servants following with wine].

                      But here they come.
 If consequence do but approve my dream,
 My boat sails freely, both with wind and stream.

Cassio: 'Fore God, they have given me a rouse° already.

Montano: Good faith, a little one; not past a pint, as I am a soldier.   55

Iago: Some wine, ho!
 [Sings.] And let me the canakin clink, clink;
              And let me the canakin clink
                 A soldier's a man;
                 A life's but a span,   60
              Why then, let a soldier drink.
      Some wine, boys!

Cassio: 'Fore God, an excellent song!

Iago: I learned it in England, where indeed they are most potent in pot-
 ting. Your Dane, your German, and your swag-bellied Hollander—   65
 Drink, ho!—are nothing to your English.

Cassio: Is your Englishman so expert in his drinking?

Iago: Why, he drinks you with facility your Dane dead drunk; he sweats
 not to overthrow your Almain; he gives your Hollander a vomit ere the
 next pottle can be filled.   70

---

31 *qualified:* Diluted.   32 *innovation:* Disturbance.   44 *pottle-deep:* Bottoms up.
46 *That . . . distance:* Very sensitive about their honor.   47 *very elements:* True representa-
tives.   54 *rouse:* Bumper.

Cassio: To the health of our general!

Montano: I am for it, lieutenant, and I'll do you justice.

Iago: O sweet England!

  [*Sings.*] King Stephen was a worthy peer;
        His breeches cost him but a crown;   75
    He held 'em sixpence all too dear,
        With that he called the tailor lown.°
    He was a wight of high renown,
        And thou art but of low degree.
      'Tis pride that pulls the country down;   80
        Then take thine auld cloak about thee.
  Some wine, ho!

Cassio: 'Fore God, this is a more exquisite song than the other.

Iago: Will you hear't again?

Cassio: No, for I hold him to be unworthy of his place that does those   85
    things.° Well, God's above all; and there be souls must be saved, and
    there be souls must not be saved.

Iago: It's true, good lieutenant.

Cassio: For mine own part—no offense to the general, nor any man of
    quality—I hope to be saved.   90

Iago: And so do I too, lieutenant.

Cassio: Ay, but, by your leave, not before me. The lieutenant is to be saved
    before the ancient. Let's have no more of this; let's to our affairs.—
    God forgive us our sins!—Gentlemen, let's look to our business. Do
    not think, gentlemen, I am drunk. This is my ancient; this is my right   95
    hand, and this is my left. I am not drunk now. I can stand well
    enough, and I speak well enough.

All: Excellent well!

Cassio: Why, very well then. You must not think then that I am drunk.

                                                                    Exit.

Montano: To th' platform, masters. Come, let's set the watch.   100

Iago: You see this fellow that is gone before.
  He's a soldier fit to stand by Caesar
  And give direction; and do but see his vice.
  'Tis to his virtue a just equinox,°
  The one as long as th' other. 'Tis pity of him.   105
  I fear the trust Othello puts him in,
  On some odd time of his infirmity,
  Will shake this island.

Montano: But is he often thus?

Iago: 'Tis evermore his prologue to his sleep:
  He'll watch the horologe a double set°   110
  If drink rock not his cradle.

Montano: It were well
  The general were put in mind of it.
  Perhaps he sees it not, or his good nature

---

77 *lown:* Rascal.   85–86 *does . . . things:* I.e., behaves in this fashion.   104 *just equinox:*
Exact equivalent.   110 *watch . . . set:* Stay awake twice around the clock.

Prizes the virtue that appears in Cassio
And looks not on his evils. Is not this true?   115

Enter Roderigo.

Iago [aside to him]: How now, Roderigo?
I pray you after the lieutenant, go!   *Exit Roderigo.*
Montano: And 'tis great pity that the noble Moor
Should hazard such a place as his own second
With one of an ingraft° infirmity.   120
It were an honest action to say
So to the Moor.
Iago: Not I, for this fair island!
I do love Cassio well and would do much
To cure him of this evil.
               (Within.) Help! help!
                                   But hark! What noise?   125

Enter Cassio, driving in Roderigo.

Cassio: Zounds, you rogue! you rascal!
Montano: What's the matter, lieutenant?
Cassio: A knave to teach me my duty?
I'll beat the knave into a twiggen° bottle.
Roderigo: Beat me?
Cassio: Dost thou prate, rogue? *[Strikes him.]*
Montano: Nay, good lieutenant!
                                             [Stays him.]

I pray you, sir, hold your hand.
Cassio: Let me go, sir,   130
Or I'll knock you o'er the mazzard.°
Montano: Come, come, you're drunk!
Cassio: Drunk?

       They fight.

Iago [aside to Roderigo]: Away, I say! Go out and cry a mutiny!
                                          Exit Roderigo.

Nay, good lieutenant. God's will, gentlemen!
Help, ho! — lieutenant — sir — Montano — sir —   135
Help, masters! — Here's a goodly watch indeed!

A bell rung.

Who's that which rings the bell? Diablo, ho!
The town will rise.° God's will, lieutenant, hold!
You'll be shamed for ever.

Enter Othello and Gentlemen with weapons.

Othello: What is the matter here?
Montano: Zounds, I bleed still. I am hurt to th' death.   140
He dies!

---

120 *ingraft:* I.e., ingrained.   128 *twiggen:* Wicker-covered.   131 *mazzard:* Head.   138 *rise:*
Grow riotous.

Othello: Hold for your lives!
Iago: Hold, hold! Lieutenant — sir — Montano — gentlemen!
 Have you forgot all sense of place and duty?
 Hold! The general speaks to you. Hold, for shame! 145
Othello: Why, how now ho? From whence ariseth this?
 Are we turned Turks, and to ourselves do that
 Which heaven hath forbid the Ottomites?
 For Christian shame put by this barbarous brawl!
 He that stirs next to carve for° his own rage. 150
 Holds his soul light; he dies upon his motion.
 Silence that dreadful bell! It frights the isle
 From her propriety.° What is the matter, masters?
 Honest Iago, that looks dead with grieving,
 Speak. Who began this? On thy love, I charge thee. 155
Iago: I do not know. Friends all, but now, even now,
 In quarter,° and in terms like bride and groom
 Devesting them for bed; and then, but now —
 As if some planet had unwitted men —
 Swords out, and tilting one at other's breast 160
 In opposition bloody. I cannot speak
 Any beginning to this peevish odds,°
 And would in action glorious I had lost
 Those legs that brought me to a part of it!
Othello: How comes it, Michael, you are thus forgot? 165
Cassio: I pray you pardon me; I cannot speak.
Othello: Worthy Montano, you were wont to be civil;
 The gravity and stillness of your youth
 The world hath noted, and your name is great
 In months of wisest censure.° What's the matter 170
 That you unlace° your reputation thus
 And spend your rich opinion° for the name
 Of a night-brawler? Give me answer to it.
Montano: Worthy Othello, I am hurt to danger.
 Your officer, Iago, can inform you, 175
 While I spare speech, which something now offends° me,
 Of all that I do know; nor know I aught
 By me that's said or done amiss this night,
 Unless self-charity be sometimes a vice,
 And to defend ourselves it be a sin 180
 When violence assails us.
Othello: Now, by heaven,
 My blood° begins my safer guides to rule,
 And passion, having my best judgment collied,°
 Assays° to lead the way. If I once stir
 Or do but lift this arm, the best of you 185

---

150 *carve for:* Indulge. 153 *propriety:* Proper self. 157 *quarter:* Friendliness. 162 *peevish odds:* Childish quarrel. 170 *censure:* Judgment. 171 *unlace:* Undo. 172 *rich opinion:* High reputation. 176 *offends:* Pains. 182 *blood:* Passion. 183 *collied:* Darkened. 184 *Assays:* Tries.

        Shall sink in my rebuke. Give me to know
        How this foul rout began, who set it on;
        And he that is approved in° this offense,
        Though he had twinned with me, both at a birth,
        Shall lose me. What! in a town of war,   190
        Yet wild, the people's hearts brimful of fear,
        To manage° private and domestic quarrel?
        In night, and on the court and guard of safety?
        'Tis monstrous. Iago, who began't?
Montano: If partially affined, or leagued in office,°   195
        Thou dost deliver more or less than truth,
        Thou art no soldier.
Iago: Touch me not so near.
        I had rather have this tongue cut from my mouth
        Than it should do offense to Michael Cassio;
        Yet I persuade myself, to speak the truth   200
        Shall nothing wrong him. This it is, general.
        Montano and myself being in speech,
        There comes a fellow crying out for help,
        And Cassio following him with determined sword
        To execute° upon him. Sir, this gentleman   205
        Steps in to Cassio and entreats his pause.
        Myself the crying fellow did pursue,
        Lest by his clamor — as it so fell out —
        The town might fall in fright. He, swift of foot,
        Outran my purpose; and I returned then rather   210
        For that I heard the clink and fall of swords,
        And Cassio high in oath;° which till to-night
        I ne'er might say before. When I came back —
        For this was brief — I found them close together
        At blow and thrust, even as again they were   215
        When you yourself did part them.
        More of this matter cannot I report;
        But men are men; the best sometimes forget.
        Though Cassio did some little wrong to him,
        As men in rage strike those that wish them best,   220
        Yet surely Cassio I believe received
        From him that fled some strange indignity,
        Which patience could not pass.°
Othello: I know, Iago,
        Thy honesty and love doth mince this matter,
        Making it light to Cassio. Cassio, I love thee;   225
        But never more be officer of mine.

        Enter Desdemona, attended.

        Look if my gentle love be not raised up!
        I'll make thee an example.

---

188 *approved in:* Proved guilty of.   192 *manage:* Carry on.   195 *partially . . . office:* Prejudiced by comradeship or official relations.   205 *execute:* Work his will.   212 *high in oath:* Cursing.   223 *pass:* Pass over, ignore.

Desdemona: What's the matter?
Othello: All's well now, sweeting; come away to bed.
    [To Montano.]
    Sir, for your hurts, myself will be your surgeon.   230
    Lead him off.

[Montano is led off.]

    Iago, look with care about the town
    And silence those whom this vile brawl distracted.°
    Come, Desdemona; 'tis the soldiers' life
    To have their balmy slumbers waked with strife.   235
                            Exit [with all but Iago and Cassio].

Iago: What, are you hurt, lieutenant?
Cassio: Ay, past all surgery.
Iago: Marry, God forbid!
Cassio: Reputation, reputation, reputation! O, I have lost my reputation! I
    have lost the immortal part of myself, and what remains is bestial. My   240
    reputation, Iago, my reputation!
Iago: As I am an honest man, I thought you had received some bodily
    wound. There is more sense in that than in reputation. Reputation is
    an idle and most false imposition; oft got without merit and lost with-
    out deserving. You have lost no reputation at all unless you repute   245
    yourself such a loser. What, man! there are ways to recover° the gen-
    eral again. You are but now cast in his mood°—a punishment more in
    policy than in malice, even so as one would beat his offenseless dog to
    affright an imperious lion. Sue to him again, and he's yours.
Cassio: I will rather sue to be despised than to deceive so good a comman-   250
    der with so slight, so drunken, and so indiscreet an officer. Drunk!
    and speak parrot!° and squabble! swagger! swear! and discourse fust-
    ian° with one's own shadow! O thou invisible spirit of wine, if thou
    hast no name to be known by, let us call thee devil!
Iago: What was he that you followed with your sword? What had he done   255
    to you?
Cassio: I know not.
Iago: Is't possible?
Cassio: I remember a mass of things, but nothing distinctly; a quarrel, but
    nothing wherefore. O God, that men should put an enemy in their   260
    mouths to steal away their brains! that we should with joy, pleasance,
    revel, and applause° transform ourselves into beasts!
Iago: Why, but you are now well enough. How came you thus recovered?
Cassio: It hath pleased the devil drunkenness to give place to the devil
    wrath. One unperfectness shows me another, to make me frankly de-   265
    spise myself.
Iago: Come, you are too severe a moraler. As the time, the place, and the
    condition of this country stands, I could heartily wish this had not so
    befall'n; but since it is as it is, mend it for your own good.

---

233 *distracted:* Excited.   246 *recover:* Regain favor with.   247 *in his mood:* Dismissed because of his anger.   252 *parrot:* Meaningless phrases.   252–53 *fustian:* Bombastic non-
sense.   262 *applause:* Desire to please.

Cassio: I will ask him for my place again: he shall tell me I am a drunkard! 270
 Had I as many mouths as Hydra,° such an answer would stop them all.
 To be now a sensible man, by and by a fool, and presently a beast! O
 strange! Every inordinate cup is unblest, and the ingredient° is a devil.

Iago: Come, come, good wine is a good familiar creature if it be well used.
 Exclaim no more against it. And, good lieutenant, I think you think I 275
 love you.

Cassio: I have well approved° it, sir. I drunk!

Iago: You or any man living may be drunk at some time, man. I'll tell you
 what you shall do. Our general's wife is now the general. I may say so
 in this respect, for that he hath devoted and given up himself to the 280
 contemplation, mark, and denotement of her parts and graces. Confess yourself freely to her; importune her help to put you in your place
 again. She is of so free,° so kind, so apt, so blessed a disposition she
 holds it a vice in her goodness not to do more than she is requested.
 This broken joint between you and her husband entreat her to splin- 285
 ter;° and my fortunes against any lay° worth naming, this crack of
 your love shall grow stronger than it was before.

Cassio: You advise me well.

Iago: I protest, in the sincerity of love and honest kindness.

Cassio: I think it freely; and betimes in the morning will I beseech the vir- 290
 tuous Desdemona to undertake for me. I am desperate of my fortunes
 if they check me here.

Iago: You are in the right. Good night, lieutenant; I must to the watch.

Cassio: Good night, honest Iago. *Exit Cassio.*

Iago: And what's he then that says I play the villain, 295
 When this advice is free I give and honest,
 Probal° to thinking, and indeed the course
 To win the Moor again? For 'tis most easy
 Th' inclining Desdemona to subdue°
 In an honest suit; she's framed as fruitful 300
 As the free elements. And then for her
 To win the Moor — were't to renounce his baptism,
 All seals and symbols of redeemèd sin —
 His soul is so enfettered to her love
 That she may make, unmake, do what she list, 305
 Even as her appetite shall play the god
 With his weak function. How am I then a villain
 To counsel Cassio to this parallel° course,
 Directly to his good? Divinity° of hell!
 When devils will the blackest sins put on,° 310
 They do suggest at first with heavenly shows,
 As I do now. For whiles this honest fool
 Plies Desdemona to repair his fortunes,
 And she for him pleads strongly to the Moor,

---

271 *Hydra:* Monster with many heads.   273 *ingredient:* Contents.   277 *approved:* Proved.
283 *free:* Bounteous.   285–86 *splinter:* Bind up with splints.   286 *lay:* Wager.   297 *Pro-*
bal: Probable.   299 *subdue:* Persuade.   308 *parallel:* Corresponding.   309 *Divinity:* The-
ology.   310 *put on:* Incite.

I'll pour this pestilence into his ear,   315
That she repeals him° for her body's lust;
And by how much she strives to do him good,
She shall undo her credit with the Moor.
So will I turn her virtue into pitch,
And out of her own goodness make the net   320
That shall enmesh them all.

Enter Roderigo.

                    How, now, Roderigo?
Roderigo: I do follow here in the chase, not like a hound that hunts, but
    one that fills up the cry.° My money is almost spent; I have been to-
    night exceedingly well cudgelled; and I think the issue will be — I shall
    have so much experience for my pains; and so, with no money at all, 325
    and a little more wit, return again to Venice.
Iago: How poor are they that have not patience!
    What wound did ever heal but by degrees?
    Thou know'st we work by wit, and not by witchcraft;
    And wit depends on dilatory time.   330
    Does't not go well? Cassio hath beaten thee,
    And thou by that small hurt hast cashiered Cassio.°
    Though other things grow fair against the sun,
    Yet fruits that blossom first will first be ripe.
    Content thyself awhile. By the mass, 'tis morning!   335
    Pleasure and action make the hours seem short.
    Retire thee; go where thou art billeted.
    Away, I say! Thou shalt know more hereafter.
    Nay, get thee gone!   *Exit Roderigo.*
               Two things are to be done:
    My wife must move for Cassio to her mistress;   340
    I'll set her on;
    Myself the while to draw the Moor apart
    And bring him jump° when he may Cassio find
    Soliciting his wife. Ay, that's the way!
    Dull no device by coldness and delay.   *Exit.* 345

ACT III

SCENE I: *Before the chamber of Othello and Desdemona.*

Enter Cassio, with Musicians and the Clown.

Cassio: Masters, play here, I will content° your pains:
    Something that's brief; and bid "Good morrow, general."

[They play.]

---

315 *repeals him:* Seeks his recall.   323 *cry:* Pack.   332 *cashiered Cassio:* Maneuvered Cassio's discharge.   343 *jump:* At the exact moment.   **Act III, Scene I.**   1 *content:* Reward.

Clown: Why, masters, ha' your instruments been in Naples,° that they
    speak i' th' nose thus?
Musician: How, sir, how? 5
Clown: Are these, I pray you, called wind instruments?
Musician: Ay, marry, are they, sir.
Clown: O, thereby hangs a tail.
Musician: Whereby hangs a tail, sir?
Clown: Marry, sir, by many a wind instrument that I know. But, masters, 10
    here's money for you; and the general so likes your music that he de-
    sires you, for love's sake, to make no more noise with it.
Musician: Well, sir, we will not.
Clown: If you have any music that may not be heard, to't again: but, as
    they say, to hear music the general does not greatly care. 15
Musician: We have none such, sir.
Clown: Then put up your pipes in your bag, for I'll away. Go, vanish into
    air, away!   *Exit Musician [with his fellows].*
Cassio: Dost thou hear, my honest friend?
Clown: No, I hear not your honest friend. I hear you. 20
Cassio: Prithee keep up thy quillets.° There's a poor piece of gold for thee.
    If the gentlewoman that attends the general's wife be stirring, tell her
    there's one Cassio entreats her a little favor of speech. Wilt thou do
    this?
Clown: She is stirring sir. If she will stir hither, I shall seem to notify unto 25
    her.
Cassio: [Do, good my friend.]   *Exit Clown.*

    Enter Iago.

              In happy time,° Iago.
Iago: You have not been abed then?
Cassio: Why, no; the day had broke
    Before we parted. I have made bold, Iago, 30
    To send in to your wife: my suit to her
    Is that she will to virtuous Desdemona
    Procure me some access.
Iago: I'll send her to you presently;
    And I'll devise a mean to draw the Moor
    Out of the way, that your converse and business 35
    May be more free.
Cassio: I humbly thank you for't.   *Exit [Iago].*
              I never knew
    A Florentine° more kind and honest.

    Enter Emilia.

Emilia: Good morrow, good lieutenant. I am sorry
    For your displeasure: but all will sure be well. 40
    The general and his wife are talking of it,
    And she speaks for you stoutly. The Moor replied

3 *Naples:* (Notorious for its association with veneral disease).   21 *quillets:* Quips.   27 *In happy time:* Well met.   38 *Florentine:* I.e., even a Florentine (like Cassio; Iago was a Venetian).

That he you hurt is of great fame in Cyprus
And great affinity,° and that in wholesome wisdom
He might not but refuse you; but he protests he loves you,   45
And needs no other suitor but his likings
[To take the safest occasion° by the front°]
To bring you in again.
Cassio: Yet I beseech you,
If you think fit, or that it may be done,
Give me advantage of some brief discourse   50
With Desdemona alone.
Emilia: Pray you come in.
I will bestow you where you shall have time
To speak your bosom° freely.
Cassio: I am much bound to you.   *Exeunt.*

SCENE II: *The castle.*

Enter Othello, Iago, and Gentlemen.

Othello: These letters give, Iago, to the pilot
And by him do my duties to the Senate.
That done, I will be walking on the works;°
Repair there to me.
Iago: Well, my good lord, I'll do't.
Othello: This fortification, gentlemen, shall we see't?   5
Gentlemen: We'll wait upon your lordship.   *Exeunt.*

SCENE III: *The castle grounds.*

Enter Desdemona, Cassio, and Emilia.

Desdemona: Be thou assured, good Cassio, I will do
All my abilities in thy behalf.
Emilia: Good madam, do. I warrant it grieves my husband
As if the cause were his.
Desdemona: O, that's an honest fellow. Do not doubt, Cassio,   5
But I will have my lord and you again
As friendly as you were.
Cassio: Bounteous madam,
Whatever shall become of Michael Cassio,
He's never anything but your true servant.
Desdemona: I know't; I thank you. You do love my lord;   10
You have known him long; and be you well assured
He shall in strangeness° stand no farther off
Than in a politic distance.°
Cassio: Ay, but, lady,
That policy may either last so long,

---

44 *affinity:* Family connections.   47 *occasion:* Opportunity; *front:* Forelock.   53 *your bosom:* Your inmost thoughts.   **Scene II.**   3 *works:* Fortifications.   **Scene III.**   12 *strangeness:* Aloofness.   13 *Than . . . distance:* Than wise policy requires.

Or feed upon such nice and waterish diet,°   15
Or breed itself so out of circumstance,
That, I being absent, and my place supplied,
My general will forget my love and service.
Desdemona: Do not doubt° that; before Emilia here
  I give thee warrant of thy place. Assure thee,   20
  If I do vow a friendship, I'll perform it
  To the last article. My lord shall never rest;
  I'll watch him tame° and talk him out of patience;
  His bed shall seem a school, his board a shrift;°
  I'll intermingle everything he does   25
  With Cassio's suit. Therefore be merry, Cassio,
  For thy solicitor shall rather die
  Than give thy cause away.

  Enter Othello and Iago [at a distance].

Emilia: Madam, here comes my lord.
Cassio: Madam, I'll take my leave.   30
Desdemona: Why, stay, and hear me speak.
Cassio: Madam, not now: I am very ill at ease,
  Unfit for mine own purposes.
Desdemona: Well, do your discretion.   *Exit Cassio.*
Iago: Ha! I like not that.
Othello: What dost thou say?   35
Iago: Nothing, my lord; or if — I know not what.
Othello: Was not that Cassio parted from my wife?
Iago: Cassio, my lord? No, sure, I cannot think it,
  That he would steal away so guilty-like,
  Seeing your coming.
Othello: I do believe 'twas he.   40
Desdemona: How now, my lord?
  I have been talking with a suitor here,
  A man that languishes in your displeasure.
Othello: What is't you mean?
Desdemona: Why, your lieutenant, Cassio. Good my lord,   45
  If I have any grace or power to move you,
  His present° reconciliation take;
  For if he be not one that truly loves you,
  That errs in ignorance, and not in cunning,
  I have no judgment in an honest face,   50
  I prithee call him back.
Othello: Went he hence now?
Desdemona: Yes, faith; so humbled
  That he hath left part of his grief with me
  To suffer with him. Good love, call him back.
Othello: Not now, sweet Desdemon; some other time.   55

---

15 *Or ... diet:* Or be continued for such slight reasons.   19 *doubt:* Fear.   23 *watch him
tame:* Keep him awake until he gives in.   24 *shrift:* Confessional.   47 *present:* Immediate.

Desdemona: But shall't be shortly?
Othello: The sooner, sweet, for you.
Desdemona: Shall't be to-night at supper?
Othello: No, not to-night.
Desdemona: To-morrow dinner then?
Othello: I shall not dine at home;
   I meet the captains at the citadel.
Desdemona: Why then, to-morrow night, or Tuesday morn,   60
   On Tuesday noon or night, or Wednesday morn.
   I prithee name the time, but let it not
   Exceed three days. I' faith, he's penitent;
   And yet his trespass, in our common reason
   (Save that, they say, the wars must make examples   65
   Out of their best), is not almost° a fault
   T' incur a private check.° When shall he come?
   Tell me, Othello. I wonder in my soul
   What you could ask me that I should deny
   Or stand so mamm'ring on.° What? Michael Cassio,   70
   That came a-wooing with you, and so many a time,
   When I have spoke of you dispraisingly,
   Hath ta'en your part — to have so much to do
   To bring him in? By'r Lady, I could do much —
Othello: Prithee no more. Let him come when he will!   75
   I will deny thee nothing.
Desdemona: Why, this is not a boon;
   'Tis as I should entreat you wear your gloves,
   Or feed on nourishing dishes, or keep you warm,
   Or sue to you to do a peculiar profit
   To your own person. Nay, when I have a suit   80
   Wherein I mean to touch your love indeed,
   It shall be full of poise and difficult weight,
   And fearful° to be granted.
Othello: I will deny thee nothing!
   Whereon I do beseech thee grant me this,
   To leave me but a little to myself.   85
Desdemona: Shall I deny you? No. Farewell, my lord.
Othello: Farewell, my Desdemon: I'll come to thee straight.
Desdemona: Emilia, come. — Be as your fancies teach you;
   Whate'er you be, I am obedient.   *Exit [with Emilia].*
Othello: Excellent wretch!° Perdition catch my soul   90
   But I do love thee! and when I love thee not,
   Chaos is come again.
Iago: My noble lord —
Othello: What dost thou say, Iago?
Iago: Did Michael Cassio, when you wooed my lady,
   Know of your love?   95
Othello: He did, from first to last. Why dost thou ask?

---

66 *not almost:* Hardly.   67 *a private check:* Even a private reprimand.   70 *mamm'ring on:*
Hesitating about.   83 *fearful:* Dangerous.   90 *wretch:* (A term of endearment).

Iago: But for a satisfaction of my thought;
    No further harm.
Othello: Why of thy thought, Iago?
Iago: I did not think he had been acquainted with her.
Othello: O, yes, and went between us° very oft.   100
Iago: Indeed?
Othello: Indeed? Ay, indeed! Discern'st thou aught in that?
    Is he not honest?
Iago: Honest, my lord?
Othello: Honest. Ay, honest.
Iago: My lord, for aught I know.
Othello: What dost thou think?
Iago: Think, my lord?
Othello: Think, my lord?   105
    By heaven, he echoes me,
    As if there were some monster in his thought
    Too hideous to be shown. Thou dost mean something:
    I heard thee say even now, thou lik'st not that,
    When Cassio left my wife. What didst not like?   110
    And when I told thee he was of my counsel
    In my whole course of wooing, thou cried'st "Indeed?"
    And didst contract and purse thy brow together,
    As if thou then hadst shut up in thy brain
    Some horrible conceit.° If thou dost love me,   115
    Show me thy thought
Iago: My lord, you know I love you.
Othello: I think thou dost;
    And, for I know thou'rt full of love and honesty
    And weigh'st thy words before thou giv'st them breath,
    Therefore these stops of thine fright me the more;   120
    For such things in a false disloyal knave
    Are tricks of custom; but in a man that's just
    They are close dilations, working from the heart
    That passion cannot rule.°
Iago: For Michael Cassio,
    I dare be sworn I think that he is honest.   125
Othello: I think so too.
Iago: Men should be what they seem;
    Or those that be not, would they might seem none!°
Othello: Certain, men should be what they seem.
Iago: Why then, I think Cassio's an honest man.
Othello: Nay, yet there's more in this.   130
    I prithee, speak to me as to thy thinkings,
    As thou dost ruminate, and give thy worst of thoughts
    The worst of words.

---

100 *went . . . us:* (I.e., as messenger).   115 *conceit:* Fancy.   123–24 *close dilations . . . rule:* Secret emotions which well up in spite of restraint.   127 *seem none:* I.e., not pretend to be men when they are really monsters.

Iago: Good my lord, pardon me:
   Though I am bound to every act of duty,
   I am not bound to that all slaves are free to.°   135
   Utter my thoughts? Why, say they are vile and false,
   As where's that palace whereinto foul things
   Sometimes intrude not? Who has a breast so pure
   But some uncleanly apprehensions
   Keep leets and law days,° and in Sessions sit   140
   With meditations lawful?
Othello: Thou dost conspire against thy friend, Iago,
   If thou but think'st him wronged, and mak'st his ear
   A stranger to thy thoughts.
Iago: I do beseech you —
   Though I perchance am vicious in my guess   145
   (As I confess it is my nature's plague
   To spy into abuses, and oft my jealousy°
   Shapes faults that are not), that your wisdom yet
   From one that so imperfectly conjects°
   Would take no notice, nor build yourself a trouble   150
   Out of his scattering and unsure observance.
   It were not for your quiet nor your good,
   Nor for my manhood, honesty, and wisdom,
   To let you know my thoughts.
Othello: What dost thou mean?
Iago: Good name in man and woman, dear my lord,   155
   Is the immediate° jewel of their souls.
   Who steals my purse steals trash; 'tis something, nothing;
   'Twas mine, 'tis his, and has been slave to thousands;
   But he that filches from me my good name
   Robs me of that which not enriches him   160
   And makes me poor indeed.
Othello: By heaven, I'll know thy thoughts!
Iago: You cannot, if my heart were in your hand;
   Nor shall not whilst 'tis in my custody.
Othello: Ha!
Iago: O, beware, my lord, of jealousy!   165
   It is the green-eyed monster, which doth mock°
   The meat it feeds on. That cuckold lives in bliss
   Who, certain of his fate, loves not his wronger;
   But O, what damnèd minutes tells he o'er
   Who dotes, yet doubts — suspects, yet strongly loves!   170
Othello: O misery!
Iago: Poor and content is rich, and rich enough;
   But riches fineless° is as poor as winter

---

135 *bound . . . free to:* Bound to tell that which even slaves are allowed to keep to themselves.
140 *leets and law days:* Sittings of the courts.   147 *jealousy:* Suspicion.   149 *conjects:*
Conjectures.   156 *immediate:* Nearest the heart.   166 *mock:* Play with, like a cat with a
mouse.   173 *fineless:* Unlimited.

    To him that ever fears he shall be poor.
    Good God, the souls of all my tribe defend   175
    From jealousy!
Othello: Why, why is this?
    Think'st thou I'ld make a life of jealousy,
    To follow still the changes of the moon
    With fresh suspicions? No! To be once in doubt
    Is once to be resolved. Exchange me for a goat   180
    When I shall turn the business of my soul
    To such exsufflicate and blown° surmises,
    Matching this inference. 'Tis not to make me jealous
    To say my wife is fair, feeds well, loves company,
    Is free of speech, sings, plays, and dances;   185
    Where virtue is, these are more virtuous.
    Nor from mine own weak merits will I draw
    The smallest fear or doubt of her revolt,°
    For she had eyes, and chose me. No, Iago;
    I'll see before I doubt; when I doubt, prove;   190
    And on the proof there is no more but this —
    Away at once with love or jealousy!
Iago: I am glad of this; for now I shall have reason
    To show the love and duty that I bear you
    With franker spirit. Therefore, as I am bound,   195
    Receive it from me. I speak not yet of proof.
    Look at your wife; observe her well with Cassio;
    Wear your eyes thus, not jealous nor secure:°
    I would not have your free and noble nature,
    Out of self-bounty,° be abused. Look to't.   200
    I know our country disposition well:
    In Venice they do let God see the pranks
    They dare not show their husbands; their best conscience
    Is not to leave't undone, but keep't unknown.
Othello: Dost thou say so?   205
Iago: She did deceive her father, marrying you;
    And when she seemed to shake and fear your looks,
    She loved them most.
Othello: And so she did.
Iago: Why, go to then!
    She that, so young, could give out such a seeming
    To seel° her father's eyes up close as oak° —   210
    He thought 'twas witchcraft — but I am much to blame.
    I humbly do beseech you of your pardon
    For too much loving you.
Othello: I am bound to thee for ever.
Iago: I see this hath a little dashed your spirits.
Othello: Not a jot, not a jot.

---

182 *exsufflicate and blown:* Spat out and flyblown.   188 *revolt:* Unfaithfulness.   198 *secure:*
Overconfident.   200 *self-bounty:* Natural goodness.   210 *seel:* Close; *oak:* Oak grain.

Iago: I' faith, I fear it has.   215
    I hope you will consider what is spoke
    Comes from my love. But I do see y' are moved.
    I am to pray you not to strain my speech
    To grosser issues° nor to larger reach
    Than to suspicion.   220
Othello: I will not.
Iago: Should you do so, my lord,
    My speech should fall into such vile success°
    As my thoughts aim not at. Cassio's my worthy friend —
    My lord, I see y' are moved.
Othello: No, not much moved:
    I do not think but Desdemona's honest.°   225
Iago: Long live she so! and long live you to think so!
Othello: And yet, how nature erring from itself —
Iago: Ay, there's the point! as (to be bold with you)
    Not to affect many proposèd matches
    Of her own clime, complexion, and degree,   230
    Whereto we see in all things nature tends —
    Foh! one may smell in such a will most rank,
    Foul disproportions, thought unnatural —
    But pardon me — I do not in position°
    Distinctly speak of her; though I may fear   235
    Her will, recoiling° to her better judgment,
    May fall to match° you with her country forms,
    And happily° repent.
Othello: Farewell, farewell!
    If more thou dost perceive, let me know more.
    Set on thy wife to observe. Leave me, Iago.   240
Iago: My lord, I take my leave.   *[Going.]*
Othello: Why did I marry? This honest creature doubtless
    Sees and knows more, much more, than he unfolds.
Iago [returns]: My lord, I would I might entreat your honor
    To scan this thing no further: leave it to time.   245
    Although 'tis fit that Cassio have his place,
    For sure he fills it up with great ability,
    Yet, if you please to hold off a while,
    You shall by that perceive him and his means.
    Note if your lady strain his entertainment°   250
    With any strong or vehement importunity;
    Much will be seen in that. In the mean time
    Let me be thought too busy° in my fears
    (As worthy cause I have to fear I am)
    And hold her free,° I do beseech your honor.   255
Othello: Fear not my government.°

---

219 *To grosser issues:* To mean something more monstrous.   222 *vile success:* Evil outcome.
225 *honest:* Chaste.   234 *position:* Definite assertion.   236 *recoiling:* Reverting.   237 *fall
to match:* Happen to compare.   238 *happily:* Haply, perhaps.   250 *strain his entertainment:* Urge his recall.   253 *busy:* Meddlesome.   255 *hold her free:* Consider her guiltless.
256 *government:* Self-control.

Iago: I once more take my leave.　　　　　　　　　　　*Exit.*
Othello: This fellow 's of exceeding honesty,
　　　And knows all qualities,° with a learned spirit
　　　Of° human dealings. If I do prove her haggard,°　　　260
　　　Though that her jesses° were my dear heartstrings,
　　　I'd whistle her off and let her down the wind
　　　To prey at fortune.° Haply, for I am black
　　　And have not those soft parts of conversation°
　　　That chamberers° have, or for I am declined　　　265
　　　Into the vale of years — yet that's not much —
　　　She's gone. I am abused, and my relief
　　　Must be to loathe her. O curse of marriage,
　　　That we can call these delicate creatures ours,
　　　And not their appetites! I had rather be a toad　　　270
　　　And live upon the vapor of a dungeon
　　　Than keep a corner in the thing I love
　　　For others' uses. Yet 'tis the plague of great ones;°
　　　Prerogatived° are they less than the base.
　　　'Tis destiny unshunnable, like death.　　　275
　　　Even then this forkèd plague° is fated to us
　　　When we do quicken.° Look where she comes.

　　　Enter Desdemona and Emilia.

　　　If she be false, O, then heaven mocks itself!
　　　I'll not believe't.
Desdemona:　　　　　How now, my dear Othello?
　　　Your dinner, and the generous° islanders　　　280
　　　By you invited, do attend your presence.
Othello: I am to blame.
Desdemona:　　　　　Why do you speak so faintly?
　　　Are you not well?
Othello: I have a pain upon my forehead, here.
Desdemona: Faith, that's with watching;° 'twill away again.　　　285
　　　Let me but bind it hard, within this hour
　　　It will be well.
Othello:　　　　　Your napkin° is too little;

　　　[He pushes the handkerchief from him, and it falls unnoticed.]

　　　Let it° alone. Come, I'll go in with you.
Desdemona: I am very sorry that you are not well.　　　*Exit [with Othello].*
Emilia: I am glad I have found this napkin;　　　290
　　　This was her first remembrance from the Moor,
　　　My wayward husband hath a hundred times
　　　Wooed me to steal it; but she so loves the token

---

259 *qualities:* Natures.　　259–60 *learned spirit Of:* Mind informed about.　　260 *haggard:* A wild hawk.　　261 *jesses:* Thongs for controlling a hawk.　　262–63 *whistle . . . fortune:* Turn her out and let her take care of herself.　　264 *soft . . . conversation:* Ingratiating manners. 265 *chamberers:* Courtiers.　　273 *great ones:* Prominent men.　　274 *Prerogatived:* Privileged. 276 *forkèd plague:* I.e., horns of a cuckold.　　277 *do quicken:* Are born.　　280 *generous:* Noble.　　285 *watching:* Working late.　　287 *napkin:* Handkerchief.　　288 *it:* I.e., his forehead.

(For he conjured her she should ever keep it)
That she reserves it evermore about her   295
To kiss and talk to. I'll have the work ta'en out°
And give't Iago.
What he will do with it heaven knows, not I;
I nothing but to please his fantasy.°

Enter Iago.

Iago: How now? What do you here alone?   300
Emilia: Do not you chide; I have a thing for you.
Iago: A thing for me? It is a common thing—
Emilia: Ha?
Iago: To have a foolish wife.
Emilia: O, is that all? What will you give me now   305
     For that same handkerchief?
Iago: What handkerchief?
Emilia: What handkerchief!
     Why, that the Moor first gave to Desdemona;
     That which so often you did bid me steal.
Iago: Hast stol'n it from her?   310
Emilia: No, faith; she let it drop by negligence,
     And to th' advantage,° I, being here, took't up.
     Look, here it is.
Iago: A good wench! Give it me.
Emilia: What will you do with't, that you have been so earnest
     To have me filch it?
Iago: Why, what is that to you?   315

     [Snatches it.]

Emilia: If it be not for some purpose of import,°
     Give't me again. Poor lady, she'll run mad
     When she shall lack it.
Iago: Be not acknown on't;° I have use for it.
     Go, leave me.   *Exit Emilia.* 320
     I will in Cassio's lodgings lose this napkin
     And let him find it. Trifles light as air
     Are to the jealous confirmations strong
     As proofs of holy writ. This may do something.
     The Moor already changes with my poison: 325
     Dangerous conceits° are in their nature poisons,
     Which at the first are scarce found to distaste,
     But with a little act upon the blood
     Burn like the mines of sulphur.

     Enter Othello.

                    I did say so.
     Look where he comes! Not poppy nor mandragora,°   330

---

296 *work ta'en out:* Pattern copied.   299 *fantasy:* Whim.   312 *to th' advantage:* Opportunely.   316 *import:* Importance.   319 *Be . . . on't:* Do not acknowledge it.   326 *conceits:* Ideas.   330 *mandragora:* A narcotic.

Nor all the drowsy syrups of the world,
Shall ever med'cine thee to that sweet sleep
Which thou owedst yesterday.
Othello: Ha! ha! false to me?
Iago: Why, how now, general? No more of that!
Othello: Avaunt! be gone! Thou hast set me on the rack.   335
    I swear 'tis better to be much abused
    Than but to know't a little.
Iago: How now, my lord?
Othello: What sense had I of her stol'n hours of lust?
    I saw't not, thought it not, it harmed not me;
    I slept the next night well, fed well, was free° and merry;   340
    I found not Cassio's kisses on her lips
    He that is robbed, not wanting° what is stol'n,
    Let him not know't, and he's not robbed at all.
Iago: I am sorry to hear this.
Othello: I had been happy if the general camp,   345
    Pioneers° and all, had tasted her sweet body,
    So I had nothing known. O, now for ever
    Farewell the tranquil mind! farewell content!
    Farewell the plumèd troop, and the big° wars
    That make ambition virtue! O, farewell!   350
    Farewell the neighing steed and the shrill trump,
    The spirit-stirring drum, th' ear-piercing fife,
    The royal banner, and all quality,
    Pride, pomp, and circumstance° of glorious war!
    And O you mortal engines° whose rude throats   355
    Th' immortal Jove's dread clamors counterfeit,°
    Farewell! Othello's occupation's gone!
Iago: Is't possible, my lord?
Othello: Villain, be sure thou prove my love a whore!
    Be sure of it; give me the ocular proof;   360
    Or, by the worth of mine eternal soul,
    Thou hadst been better have been born a dog
    Than answer my waked wrath!
Iago: Is't come to this?
Othello: Make me to see't; or at the least so prove it
    That the probation° bear no hinge nor loop   365
    To hang a doubt on — or woe upon thy life!
Iago: My noble lord —
Othello: If thou dost slander her and torture me,
    Never pray more; abandon all remorse;
    On horror's head horrors accumulate;   370
    Do deeds to make heaven weep, all earth amazed;
    For nothing canst thou to damnation add
    Greater than that.

---

340 *free:* Carefree.   342 *wanting:* Missing.   346 *Pioneers:* Sappers, laborers.   349 *big:* Stately.   354 *circumstance:* Pageantry.   355 *mortal engines:* Deadly artillery.   356 *counterfeit:* Imitate.   365 *probation:* Proof.

Iago: O grace! O heaven forgive me!
   Are you a man? Have you a soul or sense? —
   God b' wi' you! take mine office. O wretched fool,   375
   That liv'st to make thine honesty a vice!
   O monstrous world! Take note, take note, O world,
   To be direct and honest is not safe.
   I thank you for this profit;° and from hence
   I'll love no friend, sith love breeds such offense.   380
Othello: Nay, stay. Thou shouldst be honest.
Iago: I should be wise; for honesty's a fool
   And loses that it works for.
Othello: By the world,
   I think my wife be honest, and think she is not;
   I think that thou art just, and think thou art not.   385
   I'll have some proof. Her name, that was as fresh
   As Dian's visage, is now begrimed and black
   As mine own face. If there be cords, or knives,
   Poison, or fire, or suffocating streams,
   I'll not endure it. Would I were satisfied!°   390
Iago: I see, sir, you are eaten up with passion:
   I do repent me that I put it to you.
   You would be satisfied?
Othello: Would? Nay, I will.
Iago: And may; but how? how satisfied, my lord?
   Would you, the supervisor,° grossly gape on?   395
   Behold her topped?
Othello: Death and damnation! O!
Iago: It were a tedious difficulty, I think,
   To bring them to that prospect. Damn them then,
   If ever mortal eyes do see them bolster°
   More than their own! What then? How then?   400
   What shall I say? Where's satisfaction?
   It is impossible you should see this,
   Were they as prime° as goats, as hot as monkeys,
   As salt° as wolves in pride,° and fools as gross
   As ignorance made drunk. But yet, I say,   405
   If imputation and strong circumstances
   Which lead directly to the door of truth
   Will give you satisfaction, you may have't.
Othello: Give me a living reason she's disloyal.
Iago: I do not like the office.   410
   But sith I am ent'red in this cause so far,
   Pricked to't by foolish honesty and love,
   I will go on. I lay with Cassio lately,
   And being troubled with a raging tooth,
   I could not sleep.   415

---

379 *profit:* Profitable lesson.   390 *satisfied:* Completely informed.   395 *supervisor:* Specta-
tor.   399 *bolster:* Lie together.   403 *prime:* Lustful.   404 *salt:* Lecherous; *pride:* Heat.

There are a kind of men so loose of soul
That in their sleeps will mutter their affairs.
One of this kind is Cassio.
In sleep I heard him say, "Sweet Desdemona,
Let us be wary, let us hide our loves!" 420
And then, sir, would he gripe and wring my hand,
Cry "O sweet creature!" and then kiss me hard,
As if he plucked up kisses by the roots
That grew upon my lips; then laid his leg
Over my thigh, and sighed, and kissed, and then 425
Cried "Cursèd fate that gave thee to the Moor!"
Othello: O monstrous! monstrous!
Iago: Nay, this was but his dream.
Othello: But this denoted a foregone conclusion;°
'Tis a shrewd doubt,° though it be but a dream.
Iago: And this may help to thicken other proofs 430
That do demonstrate thinly.
Othello: I'll tear her all to pieces!
Iago: Nay, but be wise. Yet we see nothing done;
She may be honest yet. Tell me but this—
Have you not sometimes seen a handkerchief
Spotted with strawberries in your wife's hand? 435
Othello: I gave her such a one; 'twas my first gift.
Iago: I know not that; but such a handkerchief—
I am sure it was your wife's—did I to-day
See Cassio wipe his beard with.
Othello: If it be that—
Iago: If it be that, or any that was hers,
It speaks against her with the other proofs. 440
Othello: O, that the slave had forty thousand lives!
One is too poor, too weak for my revenge.
Now do I see 'tis true. Look here, Iago:
All my fond love thus do I blow to heaven. 445
'Tis gone.
Arise, black vengeance, from the hollow hell!
Yield up, O love, thy crown and hearted throne
To tyrannous hate! Swell, bosom, with thy fraught,°
For 'tis of aspics'° tongues!
Iago: Yet be content. 450
Othello: O, blood, blood, blood!
Iago: Patience, I say. Your mind perhaps may change.
Othello: Never, Iago. Like to the Pontic sea,°
Whose icy current and compulsive course
Ne'er feels retiring ebb, but keeps due on 455
To the Propontic and the Hellespont,
Even so my bloody thoughts, with violent pace,
Shall ne'er look back, ne'er ebb to humble love,

---

428 *foregone conclusion:* Previous experience.   429 *a shrewd doubt:* Cursedly suspicious.
449 *fraught:* Burden.   450 *aspics:* Deadly poisonous snakes.   453 *Pontic sea:* Black Sea.

Till that a capable° and wide revenge
Swallow them up.
(*He kneels.*)   Now, by yond marble heaven,   460
In the due reverence of a sacred vow
I here engage my words.
Iago: Do not rise yet.
(*Iago kneels.*)
Witness, you ever-burning lights above,
You elements that clip° us round about,
Witness that here Iago doth give up   465
The execution° of his wit,° hands, heart
To wronged Othello's service! Let him command,
And to obey shall be in me remorse,°
What bloody business ever.

[*They rise.*]

Othello: I greet thy love,
Not with vain thanks but with acceptance bounteous,   470
And will upon the instant put thee to't.
Within these three days let me hear thee say
That Cassio's not alive.
Iago: My friend is dead; 'tis done at your request.
But let her live.   475
Othello: Damn her, lewd minx! O, damn her! damn her!
Come, go with me apart. I will withdraw
To furnish me with some swift means of death
For the fair devil. Now art thou my lieutenant.
Iago: I am your own forever.   *Exeunt.* 480

SCENE IV: *The environs of the castle.*

Enter Desdemona, Emilia, and Clown.

Desdemona: Do you know, sirrah, where Lieutenant Cassio lies?°
Clown: I dare not say he lies anywhere.
Desdemona: Why, man?
Clown: He's a soldier, and for me to say a soldier lies is stabbing.
Desdemona: Go to. Where lodges he?   5
Clown: To tell you where he lodges is to tell you where I lie.
Desdemona: Can anything be made of this?
Clown: I know not where he lodges; and for me to devise a lodging, and
    say he lies here or he lies there, were to lie in mine own throat.
Desdemona: Can you enquire him out, and be edified by report?   10
Clown: I will catechize the world for him; that is, make questions, and by
    them answer.
Desdemona: Seek him, bid him come hither. Tell him I have moved° my
    lord on his behalf and hope all will be well.

459 *capable:* All-embracing.   464 *clip:* Encompass.   466 *execution:* Activities; *wit:*
Mind.   468 *remorse:* Pity.   **Scene IV.**   1 *lies:* Lives, lodges.   13 *moved:* Made pro-
posals to.

Clown: To do this is within the compass of man's wit, and therefore I'll   15
   attempt the doing of it.   *Exit.*
Desdemona: Where should I lose that handkerchief, Emilia?
Emilia: I know not, madam.
Desdemona: Believe me, I had rather have lost my purse
   Full of crusadoes;° and but my noble Moor   20
   Is true of mind, and made of no such baseness
   As jealous creatures are, it were enough
   To put him to ill thinking.
Emilia: Is he not jealous?
Desdemona: Who? he? I think the sun where he was born
   Drew all such humors° from him.

   Enter Othello.

Emilia: Look where he comes.   25
Desdemona: I will not leave him now till Cassio
   Be called to him — How is't with you, my lord?
Othello: Well, my good lady. *[Aside.]* O, hardness to dissemble! —
   How do you, Desdemona?
Desdemona: Well, my good lord.
Othello: Give me your hand. This hand is moist, my lady.   30
Desdemona: It yet hath felt no age nor known no sorrow.
Othello: This argues fruitfulness and liberal heart.
   Hot, hot, and moist. This hand of yours requires
   A sequester° from liberty, fasting and prayer,
   Much castigation, exercise devout;   35
   For here's a young and sweating devil here
   That commonly rebels. 'Tis a good hand,
   A frank one.
Desdemona: You may, indeed, say so;
   For 'twas that hand that gave away my heart.   40
Othello: A liberal hand! The hearts of old gave hands;
   But our new heraldry° is hands, not hearts.
Desdemona: I cannot speak of this. Come now, your promise!
Othello: What promise, chuck?
Desdemona: I have sent to bid Cassio come speak with you.   45
Othello: I have a salt and sorry rheum° offends me.
   Lend me thy handkerchief.
Desdemona: Here, my lord.
Othello: That which I gave you.
Desdemona: I have it not about me.
Othello: Not?
Desdemona: No, faith, my lord.
Othello: That's a fault.
   That handkerchief   50
   Did an Egyptian° to my mother give.
   She was a charmer,° and could almost read

20 *crusadoes:* Portuguese gold coins.   25 *humors:* Inclinations.   34 *sequester:* Removal.
42 *heraldry:* Heraldic symbolism.   46 *salt . . . rheum:* Distressing head cold.   51 *Egyptian:* Gypsy.   52 *charmer:* Sorceress.

The thoughts of people. She told her, while she kept it,
'Twould make her amiable° and subdue my father
Entirely to her love; but if she lost it   55
Or made a gift of it, my father's eye
Should hold her loathèd, and his spirits should hunt
After new fancies. She, dying, gave it me,
And bid me, when my fate would have me wive;
To give it her. I did so; and take heed on't;   60
Make it a darling like your precious eye.
To lose't or give't away were such perdition°
As nothing else could match.
Desdemona: Is't possible?
Othello: 'Tis true. There's magic in the web of it.
    A sibyl that had numb'red in the world   65
    The sun to course two hundred compasses,°
    In her prophetic fury sewed the work;
    The worms were hallowed that did breed the silk;
    And it was dyed in mummy° which the skillful
    Conserved of maidens' hearts.
Desdemona: I' faith? Is't true?   70
Othello: Most veritable. Therefore look to't well.
Desdemona: Then would to God that I had never seen't!
Othello: Ha! Wherefore?
Desdemona: Why do you speak so startingly and rash?
Othello: Is't lost? Is't gone? Speak, is it out o' th' way?   75
Desdemona: Heaven bless us!
Othello: Say you?
Desdemona: It is not lost. But what an if it were?
Othello: How?
Desdemona: I say it is not lost.
Othello: Fetch't, let me see't!   80
Desdemona: Why, so I can, sir; but I will not now.
    This is a trick to put° me from my suit:
    Pray you let Cassio be received again.
Othello: Fetch me the handkerchief! My mind misgives.
Desdemona: Come, come!   85
    You'll never meet a more sufficient man.
Othello: The handkerchief!
[Desdemona: I pray talk me of Cassio.
Othello: The handkerchief!]
Desdemona: A man that all his time°
    Hath founded his good fortunes on your love,
    Shared dangers with you—   90
Othello: The handkerchief!
Desdemona: I' faith, you are to blame.
Othello: Zounds!   *Exit Othello.*

---

54 *amiable:* Lovable.   62 *perdition:* Disaster.   66 *compasses:* Annual rounds.   69 *mummy:* A drug made from mummies.   82 *put:* Divert.   88 *all . . . time:* During his whole career.

Emilia: Is not this man jealous?
Desdemona: I ne'er saw this before.   95
    Sure there's some wonder in this handkerchief;
    I am most unhappy in the loss of it.
Emilia: 'Tis not a year or two shows us a man.
    They are all but stomachs, and we all but food;
    They eat us hungerly, and when they are full,   100
    They belch us.

    Enter Iago and Cassio.

                Look you — Cassio and my husband!
Iago: There is no other way; 'tis she must do't.
    And lo the happiness!° Go and importune her.
Desdemona: How now, good Cassio? What's the news with you?
Cassio: Madam, my former suit. I do beseech you   105
    That by your virtuous means I may again
    Exist, and be a member of his love
    Whom I with all the office of my heart
    Entirely honor. I would not be delayed.
    If my offense be of such mortal kind   110
    That neither service past, nor present sorrows,
    Nor purposed merit in futurity,
    Can ransom me into his love again,
    But to know so must be my benefit.
    So shall I clothe me in a forced content,   115
    And shut myself up in° some other course,
    To fortune's alms.
Desdemona: Alas, thrice-gentle Cassio!
    My advocation° is not now in tune.
    My lord is not my lord; nor should I know him,
    Were he in favor° as in humor altered.   120
    So help me every spirit sanctified
    As I have spoken for you all my best
    And stood within the blank° of his displeasure
    For my free speech! You must a while be patient.
    What I can do I will; and more I will   125
    Than for myself I dare. Let that suffice you.
Iago: Is my lord angry?
Emilia: He went hence but now,
    And certainly in strange unquietness.
Iago: Can he be angry? I have seen the cannon
    When it hath blown his ranks into the air   130
    And, like the devil, from his very arm
    Puffed his own brother — and is he angry?
    Something of moment then. I will go meet him.
    There's matter in't indeed if he be angry.

---

103 *happiness:* Good luck.   116 *shut myself up in:* Confine myself to.   118 *advocation:* Advocacy.   120 *favor:* Appearance.   123 *blank:* Bull's-eye of the target.

Desdemona: I prithee do so.   *Exit [Iago].*

                Something sure of state,°   135
    Either from Venice or some unhatched practice°
    Made demonstrable here in Cyprus to him,
    Hath puddled° his clear spirit; and in such cases
    Men's natures wrangle with inferior things,
    Though great ones are their object. 'Tis even so;   140
    For let our finger ache, and it endues°
    Our other, healthful members even to a sense
    Of pain. Nay, we must think men are not gods,
    Nor of them look for such observancy
    As fits the bridal. Beshrew me much, Emilia,   145
    I was, unhandsome warrior° as I am,
    Arraigning his unkindness with my soul;°
    But now I find I had suborned the witness,
    And he's indicted falsely.
Emilia: Pray heaven it be state matters, as you think,   150
    And no conception nor no jealous toy°
    Concerning you.
Desdemona: Alas the day! I never gave him cause.
Emilia: But jealous souls will not be answered so;
    They are not ever jealous for the cause,   155
    But jealous for they're jealous. 'Tis a monster
    Begot upon itself,° born on itself.
Desdemona: Heaven keep that monster from Othello's mind!
Emilia: Lady, amen.
Desdemona: I will go seek him. Cassio, walk here about: 160
    If I do find him fit, I'll move your suit
    And seek to effect it to my uttermost.
Cassio: I humbly thank your ladyship.

                    Exeunt Desdemona and Emilia.

    Enter Bianca.

Bianca: Save you, friend Cassio!
Cassio: What make you from home?
    How is't with you, my most fair Bianca?   165
    I' faith, sweet love, I was coming to your house.
Bianca: And I was going to your lodging, Cassio.
    What, keep a week away? seven days and nights?
    Eightscore eight hours? and lovers' absent hours,
    More tedious than the dial° eightscore times?   170
    O weary reck'ning!
Cassio: Pardon me, Bianca:
    I have this while with leaden thoughts been pressed;
    But I shall in a more continuate° time

---

135 *state:* Public affairs.   136 *unhatched practice:* Budding plot.   138 *puddled:* Muddied.
141 *endues:* Brings.   146 *unhandsome warrior:* Inadequate soldier.   147 *Arraigning ... soul:*
Indicting his unkindness before the bar of my soul.   151 *toy:* Fancy.   157 *Begot ... itself:*
Self-engendered.   170 *dial:* Clock.   173 *continuate:* Uninterrupted.

Strike off this score of absence. Sweet Bianca,

[Gives her Desdemona's handkerchief.]

Take me this work out.°
Bianca: O Cassio, whence came this?   175
This is some token from a newer friend.
To the felt absence now I feel a cause.
Is't come to this? Well, well.
Cassio: Go to, woman!
Throw your vile guesses in the devil's teeth,
From whence you have them. You are jealous now   180
That this is from some mistress, some remembrance.
No, by my faith, Bianca.
Bianca: Why, whose is it?
Cassio: I know not, sweet; I found it in my chamber.
I like the work° well; ere it be demanded,
As like enough it will, I'd have it copied.   185
Take it and do't, and leave me for this time.
Bianca: Leave you? Wherefore?
Cassio: I do attend here on the general
And think it no addition, nor my wish,
To have him see me womaned.
Bianca: Why, I pray you?   190
Cassio: Not that I love you not.
Bianca: But that you do not love me!
I pray you bring me on the way a little,
And say if I shall see you soon at night.
Cassio: 'Tis but a little way that I can bring you,
For I attend here; but I'll see you soon.   195
Bianca: 'Tis very good. I must be circumstanced.°   *Exeunt.*

ACT IV

SCENE I: *The environs of the castle.*

Enter Othello and Iago.

Iago: Will you think so?
Othello: Think so, Iago?
Iago: What,
To kiss in private?
Othello: An unauthorized kiss.
Iago: Or to be naked with her friend in bed
An hour or more, not meaning any harm?
Othello: Naked in bed, Iago, and not mean harm?   5

---

175 *Take . . . out:* Copy this embroidery for me.   184 *work:* Needlework.   196 *circum-*
stanced: Governed by circumstances.

It is hypocrisy against the devil.°
They that mean virtuously, and yet do so,
The devil their virtue tempts, and they tempt heaven.
Iago: So they do nothing, 'tis a venial slip.
　　But if I give my wife a handkerchief—　　　　　　　　　　10
Othello: What then?
Iago: Why, then 'tis hers, my lord; and being hers,
　　She may, I think, bestow't on any man.
Othello: She is protectress of her honor too;
　　May she give that?　　　　　　　　　　　　　　　　　15
Iago: Her honor is an essence that's not seen;
　　They have it very oft that have it not.
　　But for the handkerchief—
Othello: By heaven, I would most gladly have forgot it!
　　Thou said'st—O, it comes o'er my memory　　　　　　　20
　　As doth the raven o'er the infected° house,
　　Boding to all!—he had my handkerchief.
Iago: Ay, what of that?
Othello:　　　　　　　　That's not so good now.
Iago:　　　　　　　　　　　　　　　　What
　　If I had said I had seen him do you wrong?
　　Or heard him say—as knaves be such abroad　　　　　　25
　　Who having, by their own importunate suit,
　　Or voluntary dotage of some mistress,
　　Convincèd or supplied° them, cannot choose
　　But they must blab—
Othello:　　　　　　　　Hath he said anything?
Iago: He hath, my lord; but be you well assured,　　　　　30
　　No more than he'll unswear.
Othello:　　　　　　　　　　What hath he said?
Iago: Faith, that he did—I know not what he did.
Othello: What? what?
Iago: Lie—
Othello: With her?
Iago:　　　　　　　With her, on her; what you will.　　　　35
Othello: Lie with her? lie on her?—We say lie on her when they belie her.—
　　Lie with her! Zounds, that's fulsome.—Handkerchief—confessions—
　　handkerchief!—To confess, and be hanged for his labor—first to be
　　hanged, and then to confess! I tremble at it. Nature would not invest
　　herself in such shadowing passion without some instruction.° It is　　40
　　not words that shakes me thus.—Pish! Noses, ears, and lips? Is't pos-
　　sible?—Confess?—Handkerchief?—O devil!

　　(Falls in a trance.)

Iago: Work on,
　　My med'cine, work! Thus credulous fools are caught,

Act IV, Scene I.　　6 *hypocrisy . . . devil:* I.e., feigned sin instead of feigned virtue.　　21 *in-fected:* Plague-stricken.　　28 *Convincèd or supplied:* Overcome or gratified.　　39–40 *Nature . . . instruction:* My natural faculties would not be so overcome by passion without reason.

And many worthy and chaste dames even thus,   45
All guiltless, meet reproach. — What, ho! my lord!
My lord, I say! Othello!
Enter Cassio.   How now, Cassio?
Cassio: What's the matter?
Iago: My lord is fall'n into an epilepsy.
This is his second fit; he had one yesterday.   50
Cassio: Rub him about the temples.
Iago: No, forbear.
The lethargy° must have his quiet course.
If not, he foams at mouth, and by and by
Breaks out to savage madness. Look, he stirs.
Do you withdraw yourself a little while.   55
He will recover straight. When he is gone,
I would on great occasion speak with you.   *[Exit Cassio.]*
How is it, general? Have you not hurt your head?
Othello: Dost thou mock me?
Iago: I mock you? No, by heaven.
Would you would bear your fortune like a man!   60
Othello: A hornèd man's° a monster and a beast.
Iago: There's many a beast then in a populous city,
And many a civil monster.
Othello: Did he confess it?
Iago: Good sir, be a man.
Think every bearded fellow that's but yoked   65
May draw with you. There's millions now alive
That nightly lie in those unproper° beds
Which they dare swear peculiar:° your case is better.
O, 'tis the spite of hell, the fiend's arch-mock,
To lip a wanton in a secure° couch,   70
And to suppose her chaste! No, let me know;
And knowing what I am, I know what she shall be.
Othello: O, thou art wise! 'Tis certain.
Iago: Stand you awhile apart;
Confine yourself but in a patient list.°
Whilst you were here, o'erwhelmèd with your grief —   75
A passion most unsuiting such a man —
Cassio came hither. I shifted him away
And laid good 'scuse upon your ecstasy;°
Bade him anon return, and here speak with me;
The which he promised. Do but encave° yourself   80
And mark the fleers, the gibes, and notable scorns
That dwell in every region of his face;
For I will make him tell the tale anew —
Where, how, how oft, how long ago, and when
He hath, and is again to cope° your wife.   85

52 *lethargy:* Coma.   61 *hornèd man:* Cuckold.   67 *unproper:* Not exclusively their own.
68 *peculiar:* Exclusively their own.   70 *secure:* Free from fear of rivalry.   74 *in a patient list:* Within the limits of self-control.   78 *ecstasy:* Trance.   80 *encave:* Conceal.
85 *cope:* Meet.

I say, but mark his gesture. Marry, patience!
Or I shall say y'are all in all in spleen,°
And nothing of a man.
Othello: Dost thou hear, Iago?
I will be found most cunning in my patience;
But—dost thou hear?—most bloody.
Iago: That's not amiss: 90
But yet keep time in all. Will you withdraw?

                                        [*Othello retires.*]

Now will I question Cassio of Bianca,
A huswife° that by selling her desires
Buys herself bread and clothes. It is a creature
That dotes on Cassio, as 'tis the strumpet's plague   95
To beguile many and be beguiled by one.
He, when he hears of her, cannot refrain
From the excess of laughter. Here he comes.

Enter Cassio.

As he shall smile, Othello shall go mad;
And his unbookish° jealousy must conster°   100
Poor Cassio's smiles, gestures, and light behavior
Quite in the wrong. How do you now, lieutenant?
Cassio: The worser that you give me the addition°
Whose want even kills me.
Iago: Ply Desdemona well, and you are sure on't.   105
Now, if this suit lay in Bianca's power,
How quickly should you speed!
Cassio: Alas, poor caitiff!°
Othello: Look how he laughs already!
Iago: I never knew a woman love man so.
Cassio: Alas, poor rogue! I think, i' faith, she loves me.   110
Othello: Now he denies it faintly, and laughs it out.
Iago: Do you hear, Cassio?
Othello: Now he importunes him
To tell it o'er. Go to! Well said, well said!
Iago: She gives out that you shall marry her.
Do you intend it?   115
Cassio: Ha, ha, ha!
Othello: Do you triumph, Roman? Do you triumph?
Cassio: I marry her? What, a customer?° Prithee bear some charity to my
wit; do not think it so unwholesome. Ha, ha, ha!
Othello: So, so, so, so! They laugh that win!   120
Iago: Faith, the cry goes that you shall marry her.
Cassio: Prithee say true.
Iago: I am a very villain else.
Othello: Have you scored me?° Well.

---

87 *all in all in spleen:* Wholly overcome by your passion.   93 *huswife:* Hussy.   100 *unbookish:* Uninstructed; *conster:* Construe, interpret.   103 *addition:* Title.   107 *caitiff:* Wretch.   118 *customer:* Prostitute.   124 *scored me:* Settled my account (?).

Cassio: This is the monkey's own giving out. She is persuaded I will marry 125
her out of her own love and flattery, not out of my promise.

Othello: Iago beckons° me; now he begins the story.

Cassio: She was here even now; she haunts me in every place. I was t' other
day talking on the sea bank with certain Venetians, and thither comes
the bauble,° and, by this hand, she falls me thus about my neck— 130

Othello: Crying "O dear Cassio!" as it were. His gesture imports it.

Cassio: So hangs, and lolls, and weeps upon me; so shakes and pulls me!
Ha, ha, ha!

Othello: Now he tells how she plucked him to my chamber. O, I see that
nose of yours, but not that dog I shall throw it to. 135

Cassio: Well, I must leave her company.

Enter Bianca.

Iago: Before me! Look where she comes.

Cassio: 'Tis such another fitchew!° marry, a perfumed one. What do you
mean by this haunting of me?

Bianca: Let the devil and his dam haunt you! What did you mean by that 140
same handkerchief you gave me even now? I was a fine fool to take it. I
must take out the whole work? A likely piece of work that you should
find it in your chamber and know not who left it there! This is some
minx's token, and I must take out the work? There! Give it your
hobby-horse.° Wheresoever you had it, I'll take out no work on't. 145

Cassio: How now, my sweet Bianca? How now? how now?

Othello: By heaven, that should be my handkerchief!

Bianca: An you'll come to supper to-night, you may; an you will not, come
when you are next prepared for. *Exit.*

Iago: After her, after her! 150

Cassio: Faith, I must; she'll rail in the street else.

Iago: Will you sup there?

Cassio: Yes, I intend so.

Iago: Well, I may chance to see you; for I would very fain speak with you.

Cassio: Prithee come. Will you? 155

Iago: Go to! say no more. *Exit Cassio.*

Othello [comes forward]: How shall I murder him, Iago?

Iago: Did you perceive how he laughed at his vice?°

Othello: O Iago!

Iago: And did you see the handkerchief? 160

Othello: Was that mine?

Iago: Your, by this hand! And to see how he prizes° the foolish woman
your wife! She gave it him, and he hath giv'n it his whore.

Othello: I would have him nine years a-killing—A fine woman! a fair
woman! a sweet woman! 165

Iago: Nay, you must forget that.

Othello: Ay, let her rot, and perish, and be damned to-night; for she shall
not live. No, my heart is turned to stone; I strike it, and it hurts my

---

127 *beckons:* Signals. 130 *bauble:* Plaything. 138 *fitchew:* Polecat (slang for whore).
145 *hobby-horse:* Harlot. 158 *vice:* I.e., vicious conduct. 162 *prizes:* Values.

hand. O, the world hath not a sweeter creature! She might lie by an
emperor's side and command him tasks.   170
Iago: Nay, that's not your way.
Othello: Hang her! I do but say what she is. So delicate with her needle! an
admirable musician! O, she will sing the savageness out of a bear! Of
so high and plenteous wit and invention° —
Iago: She's the worse for all this.   175
Othello: O, a thousand thousand times! And then, of so gentle a condition!°
Iago: Ay, too gentle.
Othello: Nay, that's certain. But yet the pity of it, Iago! O Iago, the pity of
it, Iago!
Iago: If you are so fond over her iniquity, give her patent° to offend; for if   180
it touch not you, it comes near nobody.
Othello: I will chop her into messes! Cuckold me!
Iago: O, 'tis foul in her.
Othello: With mine officer!
Iago: That's fouler.   185
Othello: Get me some poison, Iago, this night. I'll not expostulate with her,
lest her body and beauty unprovide° my mind again. This night, Iago!
Iago: Do it not with poison. Strangle her in her bed, even the bed she hath
contaminated.
Othello: Good, good! The justice of it pleases. Very good!   190
Iago: And for Cassio, let me be his undertaker;° you shall hear more by
midnight.
Othello: Excellent good!

A trumpet.

What trumpet is that same?
Iago: I warrant something from Venice.

Enter Lodovico, Desdemona, and Attendants.

'Tis Lodovico.   195
This comes from the Duke; and see, your wife is with him.
Lodovico: God save you, worthy general!
Othello: With all my heart, sir.
Lodovico: The Duke and senators of Venice greet you.

[Gives him a letter.]

Othello: I kiss the instrument of their pleasures.

[Opens the letter and reads.]

Desdemona: And what's the news, good cousin Lodovico?   200
Iago: I am very glad to see you, signior.
Welcome to Cyprus.
Lodovico: I thank you. How does Lieutenant Cassio?
Iago: Lives, sir.
Desdemona: Cousin, there's fall'n between him and my lord
An unkind breach; but you shall make all well.   205

174 *invention:* Imagination.   176 *condition:* Disposition.   180 *patent:* License.   187 *un-*
provide: Disarm.   191 *be his undertaker:* Undertake to deal with him.

Othello: Are you sure of that?
Desdemona: My lord?
Othello [reads]: "This fail you not to do, as you will — "
Lodovico: He did not call; he's busy in the paper.
    Is there division 'twixt thy lord and Cassio?   210
Desdemona: A most unhappy one. I would do much
    T' atone° them, for the love I bear to Cassio.
Othello: Fire and brimstone!
Desdemona: My lord?
Othello: Are you wise?
Desdemona: What, is he angry?
Lodovico: May be the letter moved him;
    For, as I think, they do command him home,   215
    Deputing Cassio in his government.
Desdemona: By my troth, I am glad on't.
Othello: Indeed?
Desdemona: My lord?
Othello: I am glad to see you mad.°
Desdemona: Why, sweet Othello —
Othello: Devil!

    [Strikes her.]

Desdemona: I have not deserved this.   220
Lodovico: My lord, this would not be believed in Venice,
    Though I should swear I saw't. 'Tis very much.
    Make her amends; she weeps.
Othello: O devil, devil!
    If that the earth could teem° with woman's tears,
    Each drop she falls would prove a crocodile.°   225
    Out of my sight!
Desdemona: I will not stay to offend you.   *[Going.]*
Lodovico: Truly, an obedient lady.
    I do beseech your lordship call her back.
Othello: Mistress!
Desdemona: My lord?
Othello: What would you with her, sir?   230
Lodovico: Who? I, my lord?
Othello: Ay! You did wish that I would make her turn.
    Sir, she can turn, and turn, and yet go on
    And turn again; and she can weep, sir, weep;
    And she's obedient; as you say, obedient,   235
    Very obedient. — Proceed you in your tears. —
    Concerning this, sir — O well-painted passion!° —
    I am commanded home. — Get you away;
    I'll send for you anon. — Sir, I obey the mandate
    And will return to Venice. — Hence, avaunt!   240
                       [Exit Desdemona.]

---

212 *atone:* Reconcile.   218 *mad:* I.e., waggish.   224 *teem:* Breed.   225 *crocodile:* (Crocodiles were supposed to shed hypocritical tears to lure men to destruction).   237 *passion:* Grief.

Cassio shall have my place. And, sir, to-night
I do entreat that we may sup together.
You are welcome, sir, to Cyprus — Goats and monkeys!

Exit.

Lodovico: Is this the noble Moor whom our full Senate
    Call all in all sufficient? Is this the nature   245
    Whom passion could not shake? whose solid virtue
    The shot of accident nor dart of chance
    Could neither graze nor pierce?
Iago: He is much changed.
Lodovico: Are his wits safe? Is he not light of brain?
Iago: He's that he is; I may not breathe my censure.   250
    What he might be — if what he might he is not —
    I would to heaven he were!
Lodovico: What, strike his wife?
Iago: Faith, that was not so well; yet would I knew
    That stroke would prove the worst!
Lodovico: Is it his use?°
    Or did the letters work upon his blood   255
    And new-create this fault?
Iago: Alas, alas!
    It is not honesty in me to speak
    What I have seen and known. You shall observe him,
    And his own courses will denote him so
    That I may save my speech. Do but go after   260
    And mark how he continues.
Lodovico: I am sorry that I am deceived in him.   *Exeunt.*

SCENE II: *Within the castle.*

Enter Othello and Emilia.

Othello: You have seen nothing then?
Emilia: Nor ever heard, nor ever did suspect.
Othello: Yes, you have seen Cassio and she together.
Emilia: But then I saw no harm, and then I heard
    Each syllable that breath made up between them.   5
Othello: What, did they never whisper?
Emilia: Never, my lord.
Othello: Nor send you out o' th' way?
Emilia: Never.
Othello: To fetch her fan, her gloves, her mask, nor nothing?
Emilia: Never, my lord.   10
Othello: That's strange.
Emilia: I durst, my lord, to wager she is honest,
    Lay down my soul at stake. If you think other,
    Remove your thought; it doth abuse your bosom.°
    If any wretch have put this in your head,   15

254 *use:* Custom.   **Scene II.**   14 *abuse...bosom:* Deceive your heart.

Let heaven requite it with the serpent's curse!°
For if she be not honest, chaste, and true,
There's no man happy; the purest of their wives
Is foul as slander.
Othello: Bid her come hither. Go.   *Exit Emilia.*
She says enough; yet she's a simple bawd   20
That cannot say as much. This is a subtle whore,
A closet lock and key of villainous secrets;
And yet she'll kneel and pray; I have seen her do't.

    Enter Desdemona and Emilia.

Desdemona: My lord, what is your will?
Othello: Pray, chuck, come hither.
Desdemona: What is your pleasure?
Othello: Let me see your eyes.   25
Look in my face.
Desdemona: What horrible fancy's this?
Othello [to Emilia]: Some of your function, mistress.
Leave procreants° alone and shut the door;
Cough or cry hem if anybody come.
Your mystery, your mystery!° Nay, dispatch!   30
                                      Exit Emilia.
Desdemona: Upon my knees, what doth your speech import?
I understand a fury in your words,
[But not the words.]
Othello: Why, what art thou?
Desdemona: Your wife, my lord; your true
And loyal wife.
Othello: Come, swear it, damn thyself;   35
Lest, being like one of heaven,° the devils themselves
Should fear to seize thee. Therefore be double-damned —
Swear thou art honest.°
Desdemona: Heaven doth truly know it.
Othello: Heaven truly knows that thou art false as hell.
Desdemona: To whom, my lord? With whom? How am I false?   40
Othello: Ah, Desdemona! away! away! away!
Desdemona: Alas the heavy day! Why do you weep?
Am I the motive of these tears, my lord?
If haply you my father do suspect
An instrument° of this your calling back,   45
Lay not your blame on me. If you have lost him,
Why, I have lost him too.
Othello: Had it pleased heaven
To try me with affliction, had they rained
All kinds of sores and shames on my bare head,
Steeped me in poverty to the very lips,   50
Given to captivity me and my utmost hopes,

---

16 *serpent's curse:* (cf. Genesis 3:14).   28 *procreants:* Mating couples.   30 *mystery:* Trade,
occupation.   36 *being... heaven:* Looking like an angel.   38 *honest:* Chaste.   45 *An
instrument:* To be the cause.

I should have found in some place of my soul
A drop of patience. But, alas, to make me
A fixèd figure for the time of scorn°
To point his slow unmoving finger at!   55
Yet could I bear that too; well, very well.
But there where I have garnered up my heart,
Where either I must live or bear no life,
The fountain from the which my current runs
Or else dries up — to be discarded thence,   60
Or keep it as a cistern for foul toads
To knot and gender in — turn thy complexion there,°
Patience, thou young and rose-lipped cherubin!
Ay, there look grim as hell!
Desdemona: I hope my noble lord esteems me honest.   65
Othello: O, ay; as summer flies are in the shambles,°
     That quicken° even with blowing. O thou weed,
     Who art so lovely fair, and smell'st so sweet,
     That the sense aches at thee, would thou hadst ne'er been born!
Desdemona: Alas, what ignorant sin have I committed?   70
Othello: Was this fair paper, this most goodly book,
     Made to write "whore" upon? What committed?
     Committed? O thou public commoner!°
     I should make very forges of my cheeks
     That would to cinders burn up modesty,   75
     Did I but speak thy deeds. What committed?
     Heaven stops the nose at it, and the moon winks;°
     The bawdy wind, that kisses all it meets,
     Is hushed within the hollow mine of earth
     And will not hear it. What committed?   80
     Impudent strumpet!
Desdemona: By heaven, you do me wrong!
Othello: Are not you a strumpet?
Desdemona: No, as I am a Christian!
     If to preserve this vessel for my lord
     From any other foul unlawful touch
     Be not to be a strumpet, I am none.   85
Othello: What, not a whore?
Desdemona: No, as I shall be saved!
Othello: Is't possible?
Desdemona: O, heaven forgive us!
Othello: I cry you mercy° then.
     I took you for that cunning whore of Venice
     That married with Othello. — *[Calling.]* You, mistress,   90
     That have the office opposite to Saint Peter
     And keep the gate of hell!

     Enter Emilia.

---

54 *time of scorn:* Scornful world.   62 *turn thy complexion there:* Change thy color at that
point.   66 *shambles:* Slaughterhouse.   67 *quicken:* Come to life.   73 *commoner:* Harlot.   77 *winks:* Closes her eyes.   88 *cry you mercy:* Beg your pardon.

       You, you, ay, you!
We have done our course; there's money for your pains:
I pray you turn the key, and keep our counsel.   *Exit.*
Emilia: Alas, what does this gentleman conceive?   95
  How do you, madam? How do you, my good lady?
Desdemona: Faith, half asleep.°
Emilia: Good madam, what's the matter with my lord?
Desdemona: With who?
Emilia: Why, with my lord, madam.   100
Desdemona: Who is thy lord?
Emilia: He that is yours, sweet lady.
Desdemona: I have none. Do not talk to me, Emilia.
  I cannot weep; nor answer have I none
  But what should go by water. Prithee to-night
  Lay on my bed my wedding sheets, remember;   105
  And call thy husband hither.
Emilia: Here's a change indeed!   *Exit.*
Desdemona: 'Tis meet I should be used so, very meet.
  How have I been behaved, that he might stick
  The small'st opinion° on my least misuse?°

  Enter Iago and Emilia.

Iago: What is your pleasure, madam? How is't with you?   110
Desdemona: I cannot tell. Those that do teach young babes
  Do it with gentle means and easy tasks:
  He might have chid me so; for, in good faith,
  I am a child to chiding.
Iago: What is the matter, lady?
Emilia: Alas, Iago, my lord hath so bewhored her,   115
  Thrown such despite and heavy terms upon her
  As true hearts cannot bear.
Desdemona: Am I that name, Iago?
Iago: What name, fair lady?
Desdemona: Such as she said my lord did say I was.
Emilia: He called her whore. A beggar in his drink   120
  Could not have laid such terms upon his callet.°
Iago: Why did he so?
Desdemona: I do not know; I am sure I am none such.
Iago: Do not weep, do not weep. Alas the day!
Emilia: Hath she forsook so many noble matches,   125
  Her father and her country, and her friends,
  To be called whore? Would it not make one weep?
Desdemona: It is my wretched fortune.
Iago: Beshrew him for't!
  How comes this trick° upon him?
Desdemona: Nay, heaven doth know.
Emilia: I will be hanged if some eternal villain,   130

---

97 *half asleep:* I.e., stunned. 109 *small'st opinion:* Least suspicion; *least misuse:* Slightest misconduct. 121 *callet:* Whore. 129 *trick:* Freakish behavior.

Some busy and insinuating rogue,
Some cogging, cozening° slave, to get some office,
Have not devised this slander. I'll be hanged else.
Iago: Fie, there is no such man! It is impossible.
Desdemona: If any such there be, heaven pardon him!   135
Emilia: A halter pardon him! and hell gnaw his bones!
　Why should he call her whore? Who keeps her company?
　What place? what time? what form? what likelihood?
　The Moor 's abused by some most villainous knave,
　Some base notorious knave, some scurvy fellow.   140
　O heaven, that such companions° thou 'dst unfold,°
　And put in every honest hand a whip
　To lash the rascals naked through the world
　Even from the east to th' west!
Iago: Speak within door.°
Emilia: O, fie upon them! Some such squire he was   145
　That turned your wit the seamy side without
　And made you to suspect me with the Moor.
Iago: You are a fool. Go to.
Desdemona: Alas, Iago,
　What shall I do to win my lord again?
　Good friend, go to him; for, by this light of heaven,   150
　I know not how I lost him. Here I kneel:
　If e'er my will did trespass 'gainst his love
　Either in discourse° of thought or actual deed,
　Or that mine eyes, mine ears, or any sense
　Delighted them in any other form,   155
　Or that I do not yet, and ever did,
　And ever will (though he do shake me off
　To beggarly divorcement) love him dearly,
　Comfort forswear° me! Unkindness may do much;
　And his unkindness may defeat° my life,   160
　But never taint my love. I cannot say "whore."
　It does abhor me now I speak the word;
　To do the act that might the addition earn
　Not the world's mass of vanity could make me.
Iago: I pray you be content. 'Tis but his humor.   165
　The business of the state does him offense,
　[And he does chide with you.]
Desdemona: If 'twere no other —
Iago: 'Tis but so, I warrant.

　[Trumpets within.]

　Hark how these instruments summon you to supper.
　The messengers of Venice stay the meat: 170
　Go in, and weep not. All things shall be well.
　　　　　　　　　　　　　　Exeunt Desdemona and Emilia.

---

132 *cogging, cozening:* Cheating, defrauding.   141 *companions:* Rogues; *unfold:* Expose.
144 *within door:* With restraint.   153 *discourse:* Course.   159 *Comfort forswear:* Happiness
forsake.   160 *defeat:* Destroy.

Enter Roderigo.

How now, Roderigo?

Roderigo: I do not find that thou deal'st justly with me.

Iago: What in the contrary?

Roderigo: Every day thou daff'st me with some device,° Iago, and rather, as   175
it seems to me now, keep'st from me all conveniency° than suppliest
me with the least advantage of hope. I will indeed no longer endure it;
nor am I yet persuaded to put up in peace what already I have fool-
ishly suffered.

Iago: Will you hear me, Roderigo?   180

Roderigo: Faith, I have heard too much; for your words and performances
are no kin together.

Iago: You charge me most unjustly.

Roderigo: With naught but truth. I have wasted myself out of my means.
The jewels you have had from me to deliver to Desdemona would half   185
have corrupted a votarist.° You have told me she hath received them,
and returned me expectations and comforts of sudden respect° and
acquaintance; but I find none.

Iago: Well, go to; very well.

Roderigo: Very well! go to! I cannot go to, man; nor 'tis not very well. By   190
this hand, I say 'tis very scurvy, and begin to find myself fopped° in it.

Iago: Very well.

Roderigo: I tell you 'tis not very well. I will make myself known to Desdemona. If she will return me my jewels, I will give over my suit and repent my unlawful solicitation; if not, assure yourself I will seek satis-   195
faction of you.

Iago: You have said now.

Roderigo: Ay, and said nothing but what I protest intendment of doing.

Iago: Why, now I see there's mettle in thee; and even from this instant do
build on thee a better opinion than ever before. Give me thy hand,   200
Roderigo. Thou has taken against me a most just exception; but yet I
protest I have dealt most directly° in thy affair.

Roderigo: It hath not appeared.

Iago: I grant indeed it hath not appeared, and your suspicion is not without wit and judgment. But, Roderigo, if thou hast that in thee indeed   205
which I have greater reason to believe now than ever, I mean purpose,
courage, and valor, this night show it. If thou the next night following
enjoy not Desdemona, take me from this world with treachery and devise engines for° my life.

Roderigo: Well, what is it? Is it within reason and compass?   210

Iago: Sir, there is especial commission come from Venice to depute Cassio
in Othello's place.

Roderigo: Is that true? Why, then Othello and Desdemona return again to
Venice.

Iago: O, no; he goes into Mauritania and takes away with him the fair Des-   215

---

175 *thou . . . device:* You put me off with some trick.   176 *conveniency:* Favorable opportu-
nities.   186 *votarist:* Nun.   187 *sudden respect:* Immediate notice.   191 *fopped:* Duped.
202 *directly:* Straightforwardly.   209 *engines for:* Plots against.

demona, unless his abode be lingered here° by some accident; wherein none can be so determinate° as the removing of Cassio.

Roderigo: How do you mean removing of him?

Iago: Why, by making him uncapable of Othello's place — knocking out his brains.   220

Roderigo: And that you would have me to do?

Iago: Ay, if you dare do yourself a profit and a right. He sups to-night with a harlotry, and thither will I go to him. He knows not yet of his honorable fortune. If you will watch his going thence, which I will fashion to fall out between twelve and one, you may take him at your pleasure.   225
I will be near to second your attempt, and he shall fall between us. Come, stand not amazed at it, but go along with me. I will show you such a necessity in his death that you shall think yourself bound to put it on him. It is now high supper time, and the night grows to waste. About it!   230

Roderigo: I will hear further reason for this.

Iago: And you shall be satisfied.   *Exeunt.*

SCENE III: *Within the castle.*

Enter Othello, Lodovico, Desdemona, Emilia, and Attendants.

Lodovico: I do beseech you, sir, trouble yourself no further.

Othello: O, pardon me; 'twill do me good to walk.

Lodovico: Madam, good night. I humbly thank your ladyship.

Desdemona: Your honor is most welcome.

Othello: Will you walk, sir?
      O, Desdemona—   5

Desdemona: My lord?

Othello: Get you to bed on th' instant; I will be returned forthwith.
      Dismiss your attendant there. Look't be done.

Desdemona: I will, my lord.

      Exit [Othello, with Lodovico and Attendants].

Emilia: How goes it now? He looks gentler than he did.   10

Desdemona: He says he will return incontinent.°
      He hath commanded me to go to bed,
      And bade me to dismiss you.

Emilia: Dismiss me?

Desdemona: It was his bidding; therefore, good Emilia,
      Give me my nightly wearing, and adieu.   15
      We must not now displease him.

Emilia: I would you had never seen him!

Desdemona: So would not I. My love doth so approve him
      That even his stubbornness,° his checks,° his frowns —
      Prithee unpin me — have grace and favor in them.   20

Emilia: I have laid those sheets you bade me on the bed.

Desdemona: All's one. Good faith, how foolish are our minds!

---

216 *abode . . . here:* Stay here be extended.   217 *determinate:* Effective.   **Scene III.**   11 *in-*
continent: At once.   · 19 *stubbornness:* Roughness; *checks:* Rebukes.

    If I do die before thee, prithee shroud me
    In one of those same sheets.
Emilia: Come, come! You talk.
Desdemona: My mother had a maid called Barbary.   25
    She was in love; and he she loved proved mad°
    And did forsake her. She had a song of "Willow";
    An old thing 'twas; but it expressed her fortune,
    And she died singing it. That song to-night
    Will not go from my mind; I have much to do   30
    But to go hang my head all at one side
    And sing it like poor Barbary. Prithee dispatch.
Emilia: Shall I go fetch your nightgown?°
Desdemona: No, unpin me here.
    This Lodovico is a proper man.
Emilia: A very handsome man.   35
Desdemona: He speaks well.
Emilia: I know a lady in Venice would have walked barefoot to Palestine
    for a touch of his nether lip.
Desdemona (sings): "The poor soul sat sighing by a sycamore tree
        Sing all a green willow;
      Her hand on her bosom, her head on her knee,   40
        Sing willow, willow, willow.
    The fresh streams ran by her and murmured her moans;
        Sing willow, willow, willow;
    Her salt tears fell from her, and soft'ned the stones" —   45
    Lay by these.
        "Sing willow, willow, willow" —
    Prithee hie thee;° he'll come anon.
        "Sing all a green willow must be my garland.
      Let nobody blame him; his scorn I approve" —   50
    Nay, that's not next. Hark! who is't that knocks?
Emilia: It's the wind.
Desdemona (sings): "I call my love false love; but what said he then?
        Sing willow, willow, willow:
    If I court moe women, you'll couch with moe men."   55
    So get thee gone; good night. Mine eyes do itch.
    Doth that bode weeping?
Emilia: 'Tis neither here nor there.
Desdemona: I have heard it said so. O, these men, these men!
    Dost thou in conscience think — tell me, Emilia —
    That there be women do abuse their husbands   60
    In such gross kind?
Emilia: There be some such, no question.
Desdemona: Wouldst thou do such a deed for all the world?
Emilia: Why, would not you?
Desdemona: No, by this heavenly light!
Emilia: Nor I neither by this heavenly light.
    I might do't as well i' th' dark.   65

---

26 *mad:* Wild, faithless.   33 *nightgown:* Dressing gown.   48 *hie thee:* Hurry.

Desdemona: Wouldst thou do such a deed for all the world?

Emilia: The world's a huge thing; it is a great price for a small vice.

Desdemona: In troth, I think thou wouldst not.

Emilia: In troth, I think I should; and undo't when I had done it. Marry, I
would not do such a thing for a joint-ring,° nor for measures of lawn,   70
nor for gowns, petticoats, nor caps, nor any petty exhibition;° but, for
all the whole world—'Ud's pity! who would not make her husband a
cuckold to make him a monarch? I should venture purgatory for't.

Desdemona: Beshrew me if I would do such a wrong
For the whole world.   75

Emilia: Why, the wrong is but a wrong i' th' world; and having the world
for your labor, 'tis a wrong in your own world, and you might quickly
make it right.

Desdemona: I do not think there is any such woman.

Emilia: Yes, a dozen; and as many to th' vantage° as   80
would store° the world they played for.
But I do think it is their husbands' faults
If wives do fall. Say that they slack their duties
And pour our treasures into foreign laps;
Or else break out in peevish° jealousies,   85
Throwing restraint upon us; or say they strike us,
Or scant our former having° in despite—
Why, we have galls;° and though we have some grace,
Yet have we some revenge. Let husbands know
Their wives have sense like them. They see, and smell,   90
And have their palates both for sweet and sour,
As husbands have. What is it that they do
When they change us for others? Is it sport?
I think it is. And doth affection breed it?
I think it doth. Is't frailty that thus errs?   95
It is so too. And have not we affections,
Desires for sport, and frailty, as men have?
Then let them use us well; else let them know,
The ills we do, their ills instruct us so.

Desdemona: Good night, good night. God me such usage° send,   100
Not to pick bad from bad, but by bad mend!   *Exeunt.*

ACT V

SCENE I: *A street in Cyprus.*

Enter Iago and Roderigo.

Iago: Here, stand behind this bulk;° straight will he come.
Wear thy good rapier bare, and put it home.

---

70 *joint-ring:* Ring made in separable halves.   71 *exhibition:* Gift.   80 *to th' vantage:* Besides.   81 *store:* Populate.   85 *peevish:* Senseless.   87 *having:* Allowance.   88 *galls:*
Spirits to resent.   100 *usage:* Habits.   **Act V, Scene I.**   1 *bulk:* Projecting shop-front.

  Quick, quick! Fear nothing; I'll be at thy elbow.
  It makes us, or it mars us—think on that,
  And fix most firm thy resolution.   5
Roderigo: Be near at hand; I may miscarry in't.
Iago: Here, at thy hand. Be bold, and take thy stand.

  [Stands aside.]

Roderigo: I have no great devotion to the deed,
  And yet he hath given me satisfying reasons.
  'Tis but a man gone. Forth my sword! He dies!   10
Iago: I have rubbed this young quat° almost to the sense,°
  And he grows angry. Now whether he kill Cassio,
  Or Cassio him, or each do kill the other,
  Every way makes my gain. Live Roderigo,
  He calls me to a restitution large   15
  Of gold and jewels that I bobbed° from him
  As gifts to Desdemona.
  It must not be. If Cassio do remain,
  He hath a daily beauty in his life
  That makes me ugly; and besides, the Moor   20
  May unfold me to him; there stand I in much peril.
  No, he must die. Be't so! I hear him coming.

  Enter Cassio.

Roderigo: I know his gait. 'Tis he. Villain, thou diest!

  [Makes a pass at Cassio.]

Cassio: That thrust had been mine enemy indeed
  But that my coat° is better than thou know'st.   25
  I will make proof of thine.

  [Draws, and wounds Roderigo.]

Roderigo: O, I am slain!

  [Iago darts from concealment behind Cassio, wounds him in the leg, and exit.]

Cassio: I am maimed for ever. Help, ho! Murder! murder!

  [Falls.]
  Enter Othello.

Othello: The voice of Cassio. Iago keeps his word.
Roderigo: O, villain that I am!
Othello: It is even so.
Cassio: O, help, ho! light! a surgeon!   30
Othello: 'Tis he. O brave Iago, honest and just,
  That hast such noble sense of thy friend's wrong!
  Thou teachest me. Minion,° your dear lies dead,
  And your unblest fate hies.° Strumpet, I come.
  Forth of my heart those charms, thine eyes, are blotted. 35
  Thy bed, lust-stained, shall with lust's blood be spotted.

---

11 *quat:* Pimple; *sense:* Quick. 16 *bobbed:* Swindled. 25 *coat:* Undershirt of mail.
33 *Minion:* Mistress. 34 *hies:* Hurries on.

Exit Othello.

Enter Lodovico and Gratiano.

Cassio: What, ho? No watch? No passage?° Murder! murder!
Gratiano: 'Tis some mischance. The cry is very direful.
Cassio: O, help!
Lodovico: Hark!   40
Roderigo: O wretched villain!
Lodovico: Two or three groan. It is a heavy° night.
    These may be counterfeits. Let's think't unsafe
    To come in to the cry without more help.
Roderigo: Nobody come? Then shall I bleed to death.   45
Lodovico: Hark!

Enter Iago, with a light.

Gratiano: Here's one comes in his shirt, with light and weapons.
Iago: Who's there? Whose noise is this that cries on° murder?
Lodovico: We do not know.
Iago: Did not you hear a cry?
Cassio: Here, here! For heaven's sake, help me!
Iago: What's the matter?   50
Gratiano: This is Othello's ancient, as I take it.
Lodovico: The same indeed, a very valiant fellow.
Iago: What are you here that cry so grievously?
Cassio: Iago? O, I am spoiled, undone by villains!
    Give me some help.   55
Iago: O me, lieutenant! What villains have done this?
Cassio: I think that one of them is hereabout
    And cannot make° away.
Iago: O treacherous villains!

    [To Lodovico and Gratiano.]

    What are you there? Come in, and give some help.
Roderigo: O, help me here!   60
Cassio: That's one of them.
Iago: O murd'rous slave! O villain!

    [Stabs Roderigo.]

Roderigo: O damned Iago! O inhuman dog!
Iago: Kill men i' th' dark? — Where be these bloody thieves? —
    How silent is this town! — Ho! murder! murder! —
    What may you be? Are you of good or evil?   65
Lodovico: As you shall prove us, praise us.
Iago: Signior Lodovico?
Lodovico: He, sir.
Iago: I cry you mercy. Here's Cassio hurt by villains.
Gratiano: Cassio?   70
Iago: How is't, brother?
Cassio: My leg is cut in two.

37 *passage:* Passersby.   42 *heavy:* Cloudy, dark.   48 *cries on:* Raises the cry of.   58 *make:* Get.

Iago: Marry,° heaven forbid!
    Light, gentlemen. I'll bind it with my shirt.

    Enter Bianca.

Bianca: What is the matter, ho? Who is't that cried?
Iago: Who is't that cried?   75
Bianca: O my dear Cassio! my sweet Cassio!
    O Cassio, Cassio, Cassio!
Iago: O notable strumpet! — Cassio, may you suspect
    Who they should be that have thus mangled you?
Cassio: No.   80
Gratiano: I am sorry to find you thus. I have been to seek you.
Iago: Lend me a garter. So. O for a chair°
    To bear him easily hence!
Bianca: Alas, he faints! O Cassio, Cassio, Cassio!
Iago: Gentlemen all, I do suspect this trash   85
    To be a party in this injury. —
    Patience a while, good Cassio. — Come, come!
    Lend me a light. Know we this face or no?
    Alas, my friend and my dear countryman
    Roderigo? No — Yes, sure. — O heaven, Roderigo!   90
Gratiano: What, of Venice?
Iago: Even he, sir. Did you know him?
Gratiano: Know him? Ay.
Iago: Signior Gratiano? I cry your gentle pardon.
    These bloody accidents must excuse my manners
    That so neglected you.
Gratiano: I am glad to see you.   95
Iago: How do you, Cassio? — O, a chair, a chair!
Gratiano: Roderigo?
Iago: He, he, 'tis he!

    [A chair brought in.]

    O, that's well said;° the chair.
    Some good man bear him carefully from hence.   100
    I'll fetch the general's surgeon. *[To Bianca.]* For you, mistress,
    Save you your labor. — He that lies slain here, Cassio,
    Was my dear friend. What malice was between you?
Cassio: None in the world; nor do I know the man.
Iago [to Bianca]: What, look you pale? — O, bear him out o' th' air.   105

                              [Cassio and Roderigo are borne off.]

    Stay you, good gentlemen. — Look you pale, mistress? —
    Do you perceive the gastness° of her eye? —
    Nay, if you stare, we shall hear more anon.
    Behold her well; I pray you look upon her.
    Do you see, gentlemen? Nay, guiltiness will speak.   110
    Though tongues were out of use.

---

72 *Marry:* (From "By Mary").   82 *chair:* Litter.   99 *well said:* Well done.   107 *gastness:* Terror.

Enter Emilia.

Emilia: 'Las, what's the matter? What's the matter, husband?
Iago: Cassio hath here been set on in the dark
　　By Roderigo, and fellows that are scaped.
　　He's almost slain, and Roderigo dead.　　　　　　　　　　115
Emilia: Alas, good gentlemen! alas, good Cassio!
Iago: This is the fruits of whoring. Prithee, Emilia,
　　Go know of Cassio where he supped to-night.

　　[To Bianca.]

　　What, do you shake at that?
Bianca: He supped at my house; but I therefore shake not.　　120
Iago: O, did he so? I charge you go with me.
Emilia: Fie, fie upon thee, strumpet!
Bianca: I am no strumpet, but of life as honest°
　　As you that thus abuse me.
Emilia: 　　　　　　　　　As I? Foh! fie upon thee!
Iago: Kind gentlemen, let's go see poor Cassio dressed.　　125

　　[To Bianca.]

　　Come, mistress, you must tell 's another tale.
　　Emilia, run you to the citadel
　　And tell my lord and lady what hath happed.
　　　　　　　　　　　　　　　　　　[Exit Emilia.]
　　Will you go on afore?　　　　　　*Exeunt [all but Iago].*
　　　　　　　　This is the night
　　That either makes me or fordoes° me quite.　　　　*[Exit.]* 130

SCENE II: *A bedchamber in the castle.*

Desdemona [asleep] in her bed. Enter Othello with a light.

Othello: It is the cause, it is the cause,° my soul.
　　Let me not name it to you, you chaste stars!
　　It is the cause. Yet I'll not shed her blood,
　　Nor scar that whiter skin of hers than snow,
　　And smooth as monumental alabaster.　　　　　　　　　5
　　Yet she must die, else she'll betray more men.
　　Put out the light, and then put out the light.
　　If I quench thee, thou flaming minister,°
　　I can again thy former light restore,
　　Should I repent me; but once put out thy light,　　　　10
　　Thou cunning'st pattern of excelling nature,
　　I know not where is that Promethean heat°
　　That can thy light relume.° When I have plucked the rose,
　　I cannot give it vital growth again;
　　It needs must wither. I'll smell thee on the tree.　　　15

---

123 *honest:* Chaste. 130 *fordoes:* Destroys.　**Scene II.**　1 *cause:* Cause of justice.　8 *minister:* Servant.　12 *Promethean heat:* Divine fire.　13 *relume:* Relight.

(He kisses her.)

O balmy breath, that dost almost persuade
Justice to break her sword! One more, one more!
Be thus when thou art dead, and I will kill thee,
And love thee after. One more, and that's the last!
So sweet was ne'er so fatal. I must weep,   20
But they are cruel tears. This sorrow's heavenly;
It strikes where it doth love. She wakes.

Desdemona: Who's there? Othello?

Othello: Ay, Desdemona.

Desdemona: Will you come to bed, my lord?

Othello: Have you prayed to-night, Desdemon?

Desdemona: Ay, my lord.   25

Othello: If you bethink yourself of any crime°
Unreconciled as yet to heaven and grace,
Solicit for it straight.

Desdemona: Alack, my lord, what may you mean by that?

Othello: Well, do it, and be brief; I will walk by.   30
I would not kill thy unprepared spirit.
No, heaven forfend!° I would not kill thy soul.

Desdemona: Talk you of killing?

Othello: Ay, I do.

Desdemona: Then heaven
Have mercy on me!

Othello: Amen, with all my heart!

Desdemona: If you say so, I hope you will not kill me.   35

Othello: Hum!

Desdemona: And yet I fear you; for you're fatal then
When your eyes roll so. Why I should fear I know not,
Since guiltiness I know not; but yet I feel I fear.

Othello: Think on thy sins.

Desdemona: They are loves I bear to you.   40

Othello: Ay, and for that thou diest.

Desdemona: That death's unnatural that kills for loving.
Alas, why gnaw you so your nether lip?
Some bloody passion shakes your very frame.
These are portents,° but yet I hope, I hope,   45
They do not point on me.

Othello: Peace and be still!

Desdemona: I will so. What's the matter?

Othello: That handkerchief which I so loved and gave thee
Thou gav'st to Cassio.

Desdemona: No, by my life and soul!
Send for the man and ask him.

Othello: Sweet soul, take heed,   50
Take heed of perjury; thou art on thy deathbed.

Desdemona: Ay, but not yet to die.

---

26 *crime:* Sin.   32 *forfend:* Forbid.   45 *portents:* Signs of impending violence.

Othello: Yes, presently.°
    Therefore confess thee freely of thy sin;
    For to deny each article with oath
    Cannot remove nor choke the strong conception°   55
    That I do groan withal. Thou art to die.
Desdemona: Then Lord have mercy on me!
Othello: I say amen.
Desdemona: And have you mercy too! I never did
    Offend° you in my life; never loved Cassio
    But with such general warranty of heaven   60
    As I might love. I never gave him token.
Othello: By heaven, I saw my handkerchief in's hand!
    O perjured woman! thou dost stone my heart,°
    And mak'st me call what I intend to do
    A murder, which I thought a sacrifice.   65
    I saw the handkerchief.
Desdemona: He found it then.
    I never gave it him. Send for him hither.
    Let him confess a truth.
Othello: He hath confessed.
Desdemona: What, my lord?
Othello: That he hath used thee.
Desdemona: How? Unlawfully?
Othello: Ay.   70
Desdemona: He will not say so.
Othello: No, his mouth is stopped.
    Honest Iago hath ta'en order° for't.
Desdemona: O, my fear interprets. What, is he dead?
Othello: Had all his hairs been lives, my great revenge
    Had stomach for them all.   75
Desdemona: Alas, he is betrayed, and I undone!
Othello: Out, strumpet! Weep'st thou for him to my face?
Desdemona: O, banish me, my lord, but kill me not!
Othello: Down, strumpet!
Desdemona: Kill me to-morrow; let me live to-night!   80
Othello: Nay, if you strive—
Desdemona: But half an hour!
Othello: Being done, there is no pause.
Desdemona: But while I say one prayer!
Othello: It is too late.

      (*Smothers her.*)

[*Desdemona:* O Lord, Lord, Lord!]

      Emilia at the door.

Emilia (calls within): My lord, my lord! What, ho! my lord, my lord!   85
Othello: What noise is this? Not dead? not yet quite dead?

---

52 *presently:* At once.   55 *conception:* Belief.   59 *Offend:* Wrong.   63 *stone my heart:*
Turn my heart to stone.   72 *ta'en order:* Taken measures.

I that am cruel am yet merciful;
I would not have thee linger in thy pain.
So, so.

Emilia (within): What, ho! my lord, my lord!
Othello: Who's there?   90
Emilia (within): O, good my lord, I would speak a word with you!
Othello: Yes, 'tis Emilia. — By and by.° — She's dead. —
'Tis like she comes to speak of Cassio's death.
The noise was here. Ha! no more moving?
Still as the grave. — Shall she come in? Were't good! —   95
I think she stirs again. No. — What's best to do?
If she come in, she'll sure speak to my wife.
My wife! my wife! what wife? I have no wife.
O, insupportable! O heavy hour!
Methinks it should be now a huge eclipse   100
Of sun and moon, and that th' affrighted globe
Should yawn° at alteration.
Emilia (within):   I do beseech you
That I may speak with you, O good my lord!
Othello: I had forgot thee. O, come in, Emilia.
Soft, by and by. — Let me the curtains draw. —   105

[Closes the bed-curtains.]

Where art thou?

[Opens the door.]
Enter Emilia.

                              What's the matter with thee now?
Emilia: O my good lord, yonder's foul murder done!
Othello: What? Now?
Emilia: But now, my lord.
Othello: It is the very error° of the moon.   110
She comes more nearer earth than she was wont
And makes men mad.
Emilia: Cassio, my lord, hath killed a young Venetian
Called Roderigo.
Othello: Roderigo killed?
And Cassio killed?
Emilia: No, Cassio is not killed.   115
Othello: Not Cassio killed? Then murder's out of tune,
And sweet revenge grows harsh.
Desdemona: O, falsely, falsely murdered?
Emilia: O, Lord! what cry is that?
Othello: That? What?
Emilia: Out and alas! that was my lady's voice.   120
Help! help, ho! help! O lady, speak again!
Sweet Desdemona! O sweet mistress, speak!
Desdemona: A guiltless death I die.

---

92 *By and by:* Just a moment (addressed to Emilia).   102 *yawn:* Open, as in an earth-
quake.   110 *error:* Straying off course.

Emilia: O, who hath done this deed?

Desdemona: Nobody—I myself. Farewell.   125
Commend° me to my kind lord. O, farewell!

(She dies.)

Othello: Why, how should she be murd'red?

Emilia: Alas, who knows?

Othello: You heard her say herself, it was not I.

Emilia: She said so. I must needs report the truth.

Othello: She's like a liar gone to burning hell!   130
'Twas I that killed her.

Emilia: O, the more angel she,
And you the blacker devil!

Othello: She turned to folly, and she was a whore.

Emilia: Thou dost belie her, and thou art a devil.

Othello: She was false as water.°

Emilia: Thou art rash as fire to say   135
That she was false. O, she was heavenly true!

Othello: Cassio did top her. Ask thy husband else.
O, I were damned beneath all depth in hell
But that I did proceed upon just grounds
To this extremity. Thy husband knew it all.   140

Emilia: My husband?

Othello: Thy husband.

Emilia: That she was false to wedlock?

Othello: Ay, with Cassio. Nay, had she been true,
If heaven would make me such another world   145
Of one entire and perfect chrysolite,°
I'd not have sold her for it.

Emilia: My husband?

Othello: Ay 'twas he that told me first.
An honest man he is, and hates the slime
That sticks on filthy deeds.

Emilia: My husband?   150

Othello: What needs this iterance,° woman? I say thy husband.

Emilia: O mistress, villainy hath made mocks with love!
My husband say that she was false?

Othello: He, woman.
I say, thy husband. Dost understand the word?
My friend, thy husband; honest, honest Iago.   155

Emilia: If he say so, may his pernicious soul
Rot half a grain a day! he lies to th' heart.
She was too fond of her most filthy bargain.

Othello: Ha!

Emilia: Do thy worst.   160
This deed of thine is no more worthy heaven
Than thou wast worthy her.

---

126 *Commend:* Remember.   135 *water:* (Which is yielding).   146 *chrysolite:* (Precious topaz).   151 *iterance:* Repetition.

Othello: Peace, you were best.
Emilia: Thou hast not half the power to do me harm
     As I have to be hurt.° O gull! O dolt!
     As ignorant as dirt! thou hast done a deed—   165
     I care not for thy sword; I'll make thee known,
     Though I lost twenty lives. Help! help! Ho! help!
     The Moor hath killed my mistress! Murder! murder!

Enter Montano, Gratiano, Iago, and others.

Montano: What is the matter? How now, general?
Emilia: O, are you come, Iago? You have done well,   170
     That men must lay their murders on your neck.
Gratiano: What is the matter?
Emilia: Disprove this villain, if thou be'st a man.
     He says thou told'st him that his wife was false.
     I know thou didst not; thou'rt not such a villain.   175
     Speak, for my heart is full.
Iago: I told him what I thought, and told no more
     Than what he found himself was apt and true.
Emilia: But did you ever tell him she was false?
Iago: I did.   180
Emilia: You told a lie, an odious damnèd lie!
     Upon my soul, a lie! a wicked lie!
     She false with Cassio? Did you say with Cassio?
Iago: With Cassio, mistress. Go to, charm° your tongue.
Emilia: I will not charm my tongue; I am bound to speak: 185
     My mistress here lies murdered in her bed—
All: O heavens forfend!
Emilia: And your reports have set the murder on.
Othello: Nay, stare not, masters. It is true indeed.
Gratiano: 'Tis a strange truth.   190
Montano: O monstrous act!
Emilia: Villainy, villainy, villainy!
     I think upon't—I think I smell't!—O villainy!
     I thought so then.—I'll kill myself for grief.—
     O villainy, villainy!
Iago: What, are you mad? I charge you get you home.   195
Emilia: Good gentlemen, let me have leave to speak.
     'Tis proper I obey him, but not now.
     Perchance, Iago, I will ne'er go home.
Othello: O! O! O!   *(Falls on the bed.)*
Emilia: Nay, lay thee down and roar!
     For thou hast killed the sweetest innocent   200
     That e'er did lift up eye.
Othello: O, she was foul!

     [Rises.]

     I scarce did know you, uncle. There lies your niece,

---

164   *to be hurt:* To endure hurt.   184   *charm:* Cast a spell on.

Whose breath, indeed, these hands have newly stopped.
I know this act shows° horrible and grim.
Gratiano: Poor Desdemon! I am glad thy father's dead.   205
Thy match was mortal to him, and pure grief
Shore his old thread in twain. Did he live now,
This sight would make him do a desperate turn;°
Yea, curse his better angel from his side,
And fall to reprobation.°   210
Othello: 'Tis pitiful; but yet Iago knows
That she with Cassio hath the act of shame
A thousand times committed. Cassio confessed it;
And she did gratify° his amorous works
With that recognizance° and pledge of love   215
Which I first gave her. I saw it in his hand.
It was a handkerchief, an antique token
My father gave my mother.
Emilia: O God! O heavenly God!
Iago: Zounds, hold your peace!
Emilia: 'Twill out, 'twill out! I peace?   220
No, I will speak as liberal as the north,°
Let heaven and men and devils, let them all,
All, all, cry shame against me, yet I'll speak.
Iago: Be wise, and get you home.
Emilia: I will not.

[*Iago draws and threatens Emilia.*]

Gratiano: Fie!
Your sword upon a woman?   225
Emilia: O thou dull Moor, that handkerchief thou speak'st of
I found by fortune, and did give my husband;
For often with a solemn earnestness —
More than indeed belonged to such a trifle —
He begged of me to steal't.
Iago: Villainous whore!   230
Emilia: She give it Cassio? No, alas, I found it,
And I did give't my husband.
Iago: Filth, thou liest!
Emilia: By heaven, I do not, I do not, gentlemen.
O murd'rous coxcomb! what should such a fool
Do with so good a wife?
Othello: Are there no stones° in heaven   235
But what serves for the thunder? Precious villain!

The Moor runs at Iago [but is disarmed by Montano].
Iago kills his wife.

Gratiano: The woman falls. Sure he hath killed his wife.
Emilia: Ay, ay. O, lay me by my mistress' side.   *Exit Iago.*

204 *shows:* Appears.   208 *turn:* Act.   210 *reprobation:* Rejection by God, damnation.
214 *gratify:* Reward.   215 *recognizance:* Token.   221 *liberal as the north:* Unchecked as the
north wind blows.   235 *stones:* Bolts like those used for thunderbolts.

Gratiano: He's gone, but his wife's killed.
Montano: 'Tis a notorious° villain. Take you this weapon,   240
　　Which I have here recovered from the Moor.
　　Come, guard the door without. Let him not pass,
　　But kill him rather. I'll after that same villain,
　　For 'tis a damnèd slave.

　　Exit [Montano, with all but Othello and Emilia].

Othello:　　　　　　　　　　I am not valiant neither;
　　But every puny whipster° gets my sword.   245
　　But why should honor outlive honesty?
　　Let it go all.
Emilia:　　　　What did thy song bode, lady?
　　Hark, canst thou hear me? I will play the swan,
　　And die in music. *[Sings.]* "Willow, willow, willow."
　　Moor, she was chaste. She loved thee, cruel Moor: 250
　　So come my soul to bliss as I speak true.
　　So speaking as I think, alas, I die.

　　(She dies.)

Othello: I have another weapon in this chamber;
　　It is a sword of Spain, the ice brook's° temper.
　　O, here it is. — Uncle, I must come forth.   255
Gratiano (within): If thou attempt it, it will cost thee dear.
　　Thou hast no weapon, and perforce must suffer.
Othello: Look in upon me then and speak with me,
　　Or, naked° as I am, I will assault thee.

　　[Enter Gratiano.]

Gratiano: What is the matter?
Othello:　　　　　　　　　　Behold, I have a weapon;   260
　　A better never did itself sustain
　　Upon a soldier's thigh. I have seen the day
　　That with this little arm and this good sword
　　I have made my way through more impediments
　　Than twenty times your stop.° But O vain boast!   265
　　Who can control his fate? 'Tis not so now.
　　Be not afraid, though you do see me weaponed.
　　Here is my journey's end, here is my butt,°
　　And very seamark° of my utmost sail:
　　Do you go back dismayed? 'Tis a lost° fear.   270
　　Man but a rush° against Othello's breast,
　　And he retires. Where should Othello go?
　　Now, how dost thou look now? O ill-starred wench!
　　Pale as thy smock! When we shall meet at compt,°

---

240 *notorious:* Notable.　　245 *puny whipster:* Whippersnapper.　　254 *ice brook:* I.e., a Spanish blade, tempered in cold running water.　　259 *naked:* Disarmed.　　265 *stop:* Power to
stop.　　268 *butt:* Limit.　　269 *seamark:* Beacon, destination.　　270 *lost:* Wasted.　　271 *Man
but a rush:* Wield only a reed.　　274 *compt:* Final accounting, Last Judgment.

This look of thine will hurl my soul from heaven,   275
And fiends will snatch at it. Cold, cold, my girl?
Even like thy chastity.
O cursèd, cursèd slave! Whip me, ye devils,
From the possession of this heavenly sight!
Blow me about in winds! roast me in sulphur!   280
Wash me in steep-down gulfs of liquid fire!
Oh Desdemon! dead Desdemon! dead! Oh! Oh!

Enter Lodovico, Montano, Iago [as prisoner], and Officers; Cassio in a chair.

Lodovico: Where is this rash and most unfortunate man?
Othello: That's he that was Othello. Here I am.
Lodovico: Where is that viper? Bring the villain forth.   285
Othello: I look down towards his feet°—but that's a fable.
If that thou be'st a devil, I cannot kill thee.

[Wounds Iago.]

Lodovico: Wrench his sword from him.

[Othello is disarmed.]

Iago: I bleed, sir, but not killed.
Othello: I am not sorry neither. I'ld have thee live;
For in my sense, 'tis happiness to die.   290
Lodovico: O thou Othello that wert once so good,
Fall'n in the practice° of a damnèd slave,
What shall be said to thee?
Othello: Why, anything;
An honorable murderer, if you will;
For naught did I in hate, but all in honor.   295
Lodovico: This wretch hath part confessed his villainy.
Did you and he consent in° Cassio's death?
Othello: Ay.
Cassio: Dear general, I never gave you cause.
Othello: I do believe it, and I ask your pardon.   300
Will you, I pray, demand that demi-devil
Why he hath thus ensnared my soul and body?
Iago: Demand me nothing. What you know, you know.
From this time forth I never will speak word.
Lodovico: What, not to pray?
Gratiano: Torments will ope your lips.   305
Othello: Well, thou dost best.
Lodovico: Sir, you shall understand what hath befall'n,
Which, as I think, you know not. Here is a letter
Found in the pocket of the slain Roderigo;
And here another. The one of them imports   310
The death of Cassio to be undertook
By Roderigo.

---

286 *I . . . feet:* I.e., to see if they are cloven, like the Devil's.   292 *practice:* Plot.   297 *consent in:* Agree upon.

Othello: O villain!
Cassio: Most heathenish and most gross!
Lodovico: Now here's another discontented paper
    Found in the pocket too; and this, it seems,   315
    Roderigo mean t' have sent this damnèd villain;
    But that, belike, Iago in the nick°
    Came in and satisfied him.
Othello: O thou pernicious caitiff! —
    How came you, Cassio, by that handkerchief
    That was my wife's?
Cassio: I found it in my chamber;   320
    And he himself confessed but even now
    That there he dropped it for a special purpose
    Which wrought to his desire.
Othello: O fool! fool! fool!
Cassio: There is besides in Roderigo's letter,
    How he upbraids Iago that he made him   325
    Brave me upon the watch; whereon it came
    That I was cast;° and even but now he spake,
    After long seeming dead — Iago hurt him,
    Iago set him on.
Lodovico: You must forsake this room and go with us.   330
    Your power and your command is taken off,
    And Cassio rules in Cyprus. For this slave,
    If there be any cunning cruelty
    That can torment him much and hold him long,
    It shall be his. You shall close prisoner rest   335
    Till that the nature of your fault be known
    To the Venetian state. Come, bring away.
Othello: Soft you! a word or two before you go.
    I have done the state some service, and they know't.
    No more of that. I pray you, in your letters,   340
    When you shall these unlucky° deeds relate,
    Speak of me as I am. Nothing extenuate,
    Nor set down aught in malice. Then must you speak
    Of one that loved not wisely, but too well;
    Of one not easily jealous, but, being wrought,   345
    Perplexed° in the extreme; of one whose hand,
    Like the base Judean,° threw a pearl away
    Richer than all his tribe; of one whose subdued° eyes,
    Albeit unusèd to the melting mood,
    Drop tears as fast as the Arabian trees   350
    Their med'cinable gum. Set you down this.
    And say besides that in Aleppo once,
    Where a malignant and a turbaned Turk

---

317 *nick:* Nick of time.   327 *cast:* Dismissed.   341 *unlucky:* Fatal.   346 *Perplexed:* Distracted.   347 *Judean:* Judas Iscariot (?) (quarto reads "Indian").   348 *subdued:* I.e., conquered by grief.

Beat a Venetian and traduced the state,
I took by th' throat the circumcisèd dog   355
And smote him — thus.

(He stabs himself.)

Lodovico: O bloody period!°
Gratiano: All that's spoke is marred.
Othello: I kissed thee ere I killed thee. No way but this,
   Killing myself, to die upon a kiss.

(He [falls upon the bed and] dies.)

Cassio: This did I fear, but thought he had no weapon;   360
   For he was great of heart.
Lodovico [to Iago]:   O Spartan dog,
   More fell° than anguish, hunger, or the sea!
   Look on the tragic loading of this bed.
   This is thy work. The object poisons sight;
   Let it be hid.° Gratiano, keep the house,   365
   And seize upon° the fortunes of the Moor,
   For they succeed on you. To you, lord governor,
   Remains the censure° of this hellish villain,
   The time, the place, the torture. O, enforce it!
   Myself will straight aboard, and to the state   370
   This heavy act with heavy heart relate.

                                                        Exeunt.

357 *period:* Ending.   362 *fell:* Cruel.   365 *Let it be hid:* I.e., draw the bed curtains.
366 *seize upon:* Take legal possession of.   368 *censure:* Judicial sentence.